This book is published to accompany the television series entitled *Strictly Come Dancing* (series 7), first broadcast on BBC1 in 2009.

Executive Producer: Sam Donnelly
Series Producer: Liz Foley

BBC Books would like to thank Sam Donnelly, Jane Ashford, Martin Scott, Claire Bridgeland, Richard Halliwell, Harriet Frost, Justine Saliba, Jagdeep Sharma and the rest of the *Strictly Come Dancing* production team for all their help in compiling this book.

Strictly Come Dancing logo ™ & © BBC 2004. BBC logo ™ & © BBC 1996. Devised by the BBC and Licensed by BBC Worldwide Limited.

10 9 8 7 6 5 4 3 2 1

Published in 2009 by BBC Books, an imprint of Ebury Publishing. A Random House Group Company

Main Text by Alison Maloney
Forewords by Bruce Forsyth and Tess Daly
Copyright © Woodlands Books Ltd 2009
Alison Maloney has asserted her right to be identified as the author of this Work in accordance with the Copyright, Designs and Patents Act 1988

Series six photography by David Venni and Guy Levy © BBC 2008
Series seven photography by John Wright and Lee Strickland © BBC 2009
Strictly Come Dancing Tour photography © Alfie Hitchcock 2009
Dancing with the Stars photography of Lil' Kim, Shawn Johnson and Denise Richards © Craig Sjodin/ABC/Retna Ltd./Corbis 2009
Dancing with the Stars photography of Luke Jacobz and Prince Emanuele Filiberto of Venice and Piedmont © Getty 2009
All other photography © Fotolia.com

Design © Woodlands Books 2009
Jacket design © Woodlands Books 2009

The Random House Group Limited Reg. No. 954009

Addresses for companies within the Random House Group can be found at www.randomhouse.co.uk

A CIP catalogue record for this book is available from the British Library.

ISBN 978 1 846 07917 7

The Random House Group Limited supports the Forest Stewardship Council (FSC), the leading international forest certification organisation. All our titles that are printed on Greenpeace approved FSC certified paper carry the FSC logo. Our paper procurement policy can be found at www.rbooks.co.uk/environment

Commissioning editor: Lorna Russell
Project editor: Laura Higginson
Copy-editor: Wendy Hollas
Designer: Bobby Birchall, Bobby&Co
Production: Antony Heller

Colour origination by Altaimage, London
Printed and bound in Germany by Mohn Media GmbH

To buy books by your favourite authors and register for offers, visit www.rbooks.co.uk

Strictly Come Dancing

THE OFFICIAL 2010 ANNUAL

Alison Maloney

BBC
BOOKS

Contents

Foreword

Bruce Forsyth

Six years ago, when we took our first tentative steps on *Strictly Come Dancing*, none of us on the programme knew what a huge hit we had on our hands. Back then we had eight brave couples, who had no idea what they were letting themselves in for, and I remember the lovely Natasha Kaplinsky saying to me, as she stood at the top of the steps on the first night, 'Bruce, can you get me out of this?'

Since then the show and the audience has grown and the number of contestants has doubled to 16. The more the merrier, I say. The more celebrities in the mix, the more interest there is. It also gives us a few more of the not-so-good dancers to entertain us and maybe provide us with a few laughs.

The exciting thing is that, after the first month, we start to see people improving immensely and then you can see who is going to do very well. You see them sorting themselves out and they work so hard to make that happen, none more so than in the last series.

After the stunning achievements of Alesha Dixon, and the nail-biting final between Alesha and Matt Di Angelo, series five looked, once again, like a hard act to follow. But series six turned out to be just as amazing and entertaining to watch, for so many reasons.

To start with we had a wonderful bunch of celebrities – how lucky we were to get such great names and sparkling personalities. And rather than having one or two front-runners, there were four potential winners left at the end so the quarter-finals were the most closely fought we've ever had.

Tom Chambers was excellent, and his showdance was one of the most entertaining I've seen. He was someone who has always wanted to dance and when given the chance, he surpassed expectations and surprised himself at what he was able to do; in the same way that Alesha, the year before, had proved to herself that she was a hugely talented dancer – something she had wanted to know all her life.

Lisa Snowdon got off to a shaky start but how she improved! She and Brendan Cole were a great team and to get a maximum judges' score of 80 in the final was incredible. Rachel Stevens was unforgettable and her tango with Vincent Simone in the semi-final was a real showstopper. Rugby player Austin Healey was fantastic and, again, could easily have been the one lifting the trophy.

Speaking as an older man myself, I'm all for the older contestants putting up a good show so I particularly enjoyed watching Don Warrington and thought Cherie Lunghi was outstanding. The Latin wasn't always her strong point but in the ballroom dances she was superb. If there hadn't been as much Latin, I think she could have won it.

Then we come to John Sergeant. What can you say about John Sergeant? The whole thing went on week after week and it was very funny. He had some wonderful comments and he and the beautiful Kristina were quite a team. Sometimes they went from bad to worse, and the paso doble is something we'll never forget – it was a dancing sensation. What made me laugh in the final was that I'm sure John still thought he had won. He was right in the middle of all the people on the stage and he stepped forward like he was

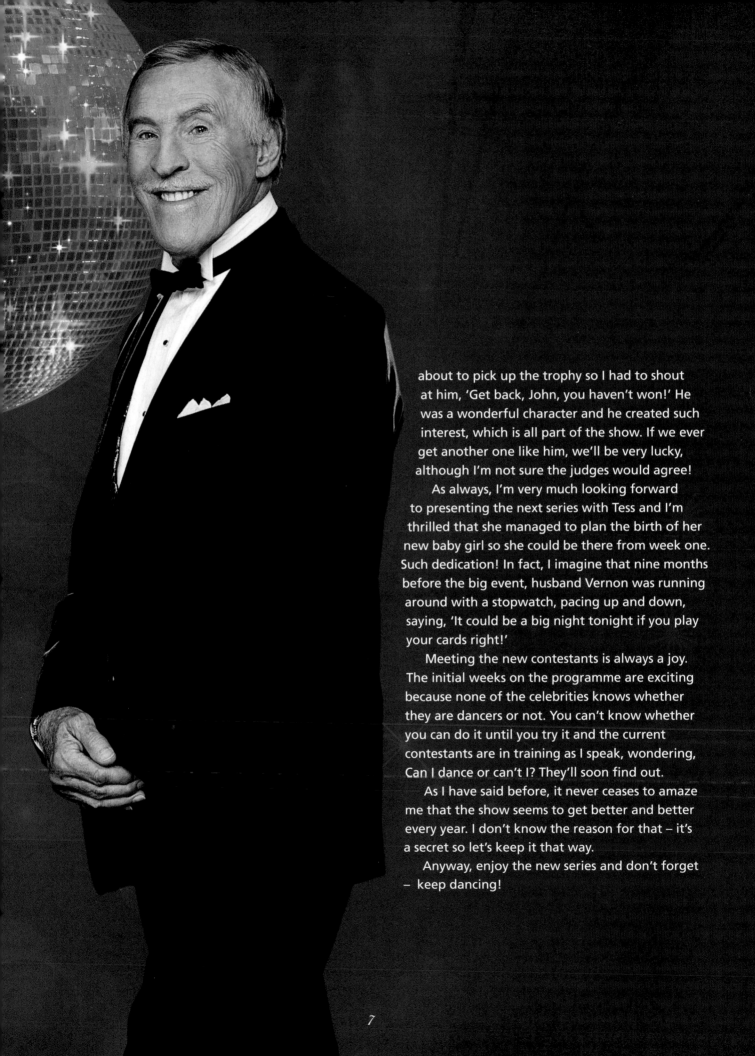

about to pick up the trophy so I had to shout
at him, 'Get back, John, you haven't won!' He
was a wonderful character and he created such
interest, which is all part of the show. If we ever
get another one like him, we'll be very lucky,
although I'm not sure the judges would agree!

As always, I'm very much looking forward
to presenting the next series with Tess and I'm
thrilled that she managed to plan the birth of her
new baby girl so she could be there from week one.
Such dedication! In fact, I imagine that nine months
before the big event, husband Vernon was running
around with a stopwatch, pacing up and down,
saying, 'It could be a big night tonight if you play
your cards right!'

Meeting the new contestants is always a joy.
The initial weeks on the programme are exciting
because none of the celebrities knows whether
they are dancers or not. You can't know whether
you can do it until you try it and the current
contestants are in training as I speak, wondering,
Can I dance or can't I? They'll soon find out.

As I have said before, it never ceases to amaze
me that the show seems to get better and better
every year. I don't know the reason for that – it's
a secret so let's keep it that way.

Anyway, enjoy the new series and don't forget
– keep dancing!

Tess Daly

O K, girls, let's talk frocks! One of the many things I love about *Strictly* is that I get to wear a fabulous dress on a Saturday night and have my hair and make-up done. For me that's a total treat because, with two young children, beauty regimes don't figure in my daily life as much as they once did!

While I'm in the make-up chair I try and put my feet up but more often than not I'm juggling a script and being briefed on last-minute changes, or stories about our dancers, or whether someone is injured, so there's always something happening.

The *Strictly* costume experts are usually very busy making clothes for the dancers, so mine often come from a different array of designers. We beg, borrow or buy and I work closely with the talented stylist Annabel Kerman, who is great. She has really changed the way that I dress and thanks to her my look has really evolved with the show. At the start of the last series I'd got my flat tummy back after the birth of my first baby, Phoebe, so we decided to go for the 'bodycon' look, the whole Hervé Léger mode, with figure-skimming frocks. Unfortunately that didn't turn out to be the best decision because I found out I was pregnant part way through the series – so all those figure-hugging dresses that we'd already acquired, and couldn't be returned, got more and more difficult to squeeze into! By the end of the series I was longing for the Empire line that I'd stuck to in previous years. They're a lot more forgiving.

It was quite stressful trying to hide the baby bump towards the end of the series. I didn't want to announce I was pregnant until I knew everything was OK, so I was desperately trying to hold it all in.

I adored the gold-sequinned dress that I wore for the final. This time it was made for me by the *Strictly* costume department and I was so looking forward to wearing it. Unfortunately, by that stage I was about 16 weeks pregnant so I had quite a big tummy, which wasn't easy to hide in skin-tight gold sequins.

My only wish is that these gorgeous gowns were mine to keep. At the end of the night they go to be stored in the BBC wardrobe somewhere. They have wardrobe sales to raise funds at the end of the year so I hope they all go to good homes.

Some of the designers lend us dresses in sample sizes, which fit their catwalk models, but I have just had my second daughter, Amber, so the thought of trying to squeeze into one of those is pretty daunting.

My four year old, Phoebe, is even more excited than me about the new series. When I told her I was seeing Bruce for a *Strictly* meeting last week she literally screamed, jumped up and down and went and got her sparkly *Strictly* dress. Her favourite thing in the world is just to dance. Daddy DJ gets on the decks at home and she puts on her dancing clothes and just does her thing. She thinks they've been waiting for me to have the baby before they could come back on air, but I told her, 'No, Mummy just timed it well!'

Series six was brilliant, yet again. I loved watching Austin Healey because he always came out with some stunt or other. He was a phenomenal dancer, took to it like a duck to water, and I really think he went too soon. And he had those fabulous arms – the legendary guns!

Rachel and Vincent had the sizzling chemistry and their tango was gorgeous, literally causing goose pimples every time they danced it. And who could forget Mark Foster, for that chest!

The girls were wonderful too. Christine was lovely. Lisa did so well and really learned to dance. Cherie Lunghi – wow! What a pair of legs and what a classy

lady. I was really sad when she went. I took it badly because I'd really got behind her and she was such an inspiration for the mature woman. She knocked spots off all the younger ones and she was such a laugh and such a pleasure to be around.

John Sergeant was hilarious. He used to brief me about his gags. He had a joke ready every week, he had such a great sense of humour, but he'd take me to one side and say, 'OK, Tess, this is how it works' I'd say, 'Don't tell me too much. Let's make it a surprise.' He looked for the laugh in each situation; he was a total comedian.

Watching Tom go all the way and win it was brilliant. On the night he deserved it because he really pulled it out of the bag. It was wonderful to see Camilla win because she wanted it so badly, and I'm devastated that she has left the show. She's been with us since day one and she's really one of the gang so I'm going to miss her loads.

This year I'll have even more sympathy for the *Strictly* contestants after performing an American smooth with Anton on last year's Children In Need. I really enjoyed the training because Anton is a total star and a laugh a minute. To be honest, we laughed more than we danced. He'd throw me in the air and I was terrified half the time! I was doing all these gravity-defying stunts where I'd find myself whipped above his head and held aloft and I did get quite fit. I was in the early stages of my pregnancy and hadn't even had the first scan, so I hadn't told a soul. Anton was whirling me around in Viennese-waltz style and I felt really sick half the time. I kept having to sit down, have a drink of water and put my head in my hands – I'm sure he thought I was a complete wimp! That aside, I loved every minute of it. He was a total professional and the poor darling had a challenge on his hands with me – two left feet.

On the night of Children In Need, I felt so, so sick. A combination of morning sickness, nerves and flu made me feel terrible and after my dance I had to sit down for 20 minutes. I went completely green. I've never been more nervous in my life.

As always, I can't wait for this series and I'm very excited about the new format. It will be like *Strictly* the movie, every Saturday night. I love seeing how the dynamics play themselves out. We all get to know the characters in the show so well because we spend four months with them and see their transformation as they learn to dance and really embrace it, sometimes to the point of obsession. And it's great to see how they all mesh as a group and it's fun to be a part of all that. It's like being on a school trip backstage, every week.

And, of course, I get to wear the gorgeous dresses again. We girls never get tired of dressing up!

SCD Expert

Are you a foxtrot fanatic or a quickstep quiz star?
Find out how well you know your *Strictly Come Dancing* with our fun questions:

1 Which professional dancer jived his way to the trophy with ex-*EastEnder* Jill Halfpenny in series two?

2 Camilla Dallerup won series six with Tom Chambers, but who was her partner in series four?

3 What prop do many couples choose for the paso doble?

4 Who was the first male celebrity to wear a kilt on the show?

5 How many former *EastEnders* have graced the dance floor since the show began?

6 Which couple chose life-sized puppets as props in their showdance?

7 Which former gymnast wowed the audience with cartwheels and splits in series five?

8 Who was the first celebrity to receive a perfect 40?

9 Which series saw the first dance-off?

10 Who was left with a bleeding nose in his series-three paso doble, prompting Len to comment, 'You look as though you've been in a bullfight!'

11 Brendan Cole used his bad-boy image to his advantage when he choreographed a jive where his partner wagged a finger to tell him off for an illegal lift in series four. Which actress was he dancing with?

12 Who was the first sporting personality to reach the final?

13 Whose series-four top-hat-and-tails routine was dismissed by Craig with the words, 'Hat, why bother? Waltz, why bother?'

14 Which cheeky celeb said, 'They couldn't have given me a better partner than Lilia – she wears next to nothing!'?

15 Whose series-two quickstep impressed Len into commenting, 'It was like walking in the air'?

16 Who was Anton Du Beke's first celeb partner?

17 Who was Len talking about when he said the fellow judge 'reminds me of my first wife. I'd do twenty things good and one thing bad and she was on me'?

18 Which male celeb messed up two dances in the quarter-finals but danced a stunning semi-final waltz, which Bruno called, 'The biggest comeback since Judy Garland – a star is born'?

19 Who is Darren Bennett's professional dance partner?

20 Which dance was introduced to Britain by Pierre Lavelle, who added triple step to distinguish it from the rumba after a visit to Cuba in 1952?

21 Fill in the missing words from Bruno's appraisal of Andrew Castle after the group dance in week one of series six: 'Andrew, there was one step you did where you looked like you were about to pass —'

22 Which couple were allowed to start again when their microphones got tangled up in series four?

23 Which two celebs got a one from Craig in series six?

24 Who danced the hilarious paso with Chris Parker in series one?

25 Which professional got Tess on to the dance floor for 2008's Children In Need?

26 Which professional dancer slipped in his showdance during the series three final?

27 What do Tess and Bruce say at the end of each programme?

28 What percentage of the American smooth must be in hold?

29 Name the three professionals who joined the show in series six.

30 Which milestone birthday did Bruce Forsyth celebrate in February 2008?

Strictly Bingo

Fancy making Saturday nights even more fun? How about a bit of ballroom bingo or Latin lotto?

Below are four bingo cards listing various events from the show. Each player should pick a card and mark off the squared boxes as they go. **When you have ticked all your boxes, shout 'Cha-cha-cha!'.** You can play on any episode and, if you use a pencil, you can always rub your ticks out and start again.

Strictly Bingo Card 1

- ◯ Craig says 'Darling'
- ◯ Any judge awards a ten
- ◯ A wardrobe malfunction during a dance
- ◯ Alesha awards an eight
- ◯ Bruno leaps to his feet
- ◯ Bruce mentions an item of the dancers' clothing

Strictly Bingo Card 2

- ◯ Len says 'Se-VEN'
- ◯ Craig says 'Dull, dull, dull'
- ◯ A contestant hugs their partner after scores
- ◯ Bruno awards a six
- ◯ Any judge mentions a stumble or mistake
- ◯ Anyone gets a ten

Strictly Bingo Card 3

- ◯ Brendan stands up for his partner
- ◯ Alesha says 'Fantastic'
- ◯ A contestant injures themselves
- ◯ Bruce says 'you're my favourite'
- ◯ Len says 'Good job'
- ◯ Anyone gets a four

Strictly Bingo Card 4

- ◯ Bruno leaps to his feet
- ◯ Craig says 'Fab-U-Lous'
- ◯ Judges row
- ◯ Bruno awards a nine
- ◯ Bruce says 'We'll see'
- ◯ Len says 'Se-VEN'

THE SERIES 6 STORY

EPISODE 1

Boys' Night Out

With 16 celebrities to fit in, the men gallantly took to the dance floor first. Despite his nerves, Tom Chambers kicked off proceedings with a cha cha cha, which left Bruno purring about tomcats and Arlene fluttering about 'magic movement in those hips'.

Albert Square Dance

Rugby player Austin Healey kicked off his *Strictly* campaign with a waltz that shocked Craig with its 'graceful, elegant lines', had Arlene raving, 'You're gorgeous,' and Len declaring it 'the best first dance for a man that I have ever seen!' After dropping Flavia in training, *EastEnder* Phil Daniels produced a first dance that Craig called 'common' and waltzed his way out of the competition.

EPISODE 2

Gary Cooks Up a Storm

Celebrity chef Gary Rhodes told partner Karen Hardy, 'I want everything to be perfect because that's the way I am in the kitchen.' But his bizarre cha cha cha failed to impress and left Karen in tears when Bruno compared them to 'the mad chef from *The Muppet Show* and Miss Piggy', and Craig gave them a one.

Here Come the Girls

After a successful group dance in week one, the ladies got their chance to compete. Christine couldn't believe her luck when her 'elegant' foxtrot went down a treat, and even Craig 'said something kind of positive!' Her respectable score of 27 was trumped by Cherie Lunghi's top-scoring foxtrot (with 32), which Len called 'the dance of the night'.

Brendan Breaks the Ice

Lisa Snowdon and Brendan Cole got off to a bumpy start when she needed an ice pack after he accidentally hit her in the face during the group-dance training. And their debut salsa didn't help matters, scoring a mere 22. By contrast, Rachel Stevens sizzled in her 'stunning sexy salsa' and landed an impressive 31.

The Ender the Line

It was a bad fortnight for former residents of Albert Square. With Phil gone, Jessie Wallace's salsa left the judges flat, giving her the lowest score of 20, and despite a foxtrot that Craig kindly remarked 'wasn't a complete disaster', Gillian Taylforth shared a dance-off with model Jodie Kidd and trotted off.

You've Been Tangoed

Newcomer Hayley Holt felt the full power of Olympic swimmer Mark Foster when he whacked her on the head during tango training, reducing her to tears. 'It wasn't the pain. I was just at the end of my tether,' she explained. Despite what Craig called 'a vast improvement', the couple ended up in the dance-off against Gary and Karen.

Hit the Rhode, Gary

After surviving last week's dance-off by what Len called a 'gnat's scrotum', Don Warrington delivered a 'masterful' tango, which gained him third place on the leader board with 30. Gary lost his cool with Karen during training and then delivered a jive that Bruno said 'had more holes than the surface of the moon', before going back to his kitchen.

EPISODE 3

The Boys Are Back in Town

Austin went down a storm with the ladies in a cut-off shirt that showed his 'guns', and he added a few cheeky moves, winking at the judges as he shimmied towards them. 'I don't like rugby players winking at me,' moaned Len but Arlene loved it and declared, 'Beat that if you can!' The rugby star led the scrum once more with 34.

EPISODE 4

Fame at Last

Week four was ladies' night again but the boys made sure they made their mark. It was wild wigs and legwarmers all round after Austin suggested they dress up for the *Fame* group-dance training in the appropriate clothing. And having thrown a strop over the judges' comments a fortnight before, Brendan still wasn't happy with Lisa's great rumba score of 32, complaining, 'I've seen nines for a lot less.'

Latin Love-In

After her triumphant debut at the top of the table, actress Cherie Lunghi kissed partner James and declared, 'He's my rock!' She followed that with a sexy rumba and left Arlene gasping, 'I have never seen James dance so tenderly for as long as I have known him.' Poor Ola! Craig and Arlene fell out when he accused her of exaggerating over Heather's 'flat' quickstep. But Heather's dance partner still planted a kiss on her after she said, 'Brian could wear anything and look fabulous!'

Tears and Tiaras

Rachel broke down in training, leaving a concerned Vincent asking, 'Did I push you too much?' But she recovered on the night and her 'light, tight, bright' quickstep left her in second place behind Cherie. The curse of the Queen Vic struck again and Jessie Wallace was reduced to tears after Arlene said she 'looked like she was on the football field' during her quickstep. After a dance-off against Heather, she was out.

EPISODE 5

Andrew's Double Fault

The girls were up against the boys for the first time in week five when former tennis player Andrew Castle's American proved not to be too smooth. Having chosen the deeply apt

track 'You Know I'm No Good', he fumbled the lift and nearly dropped Ola, then finished by saying, 'That was rotten.' The judges agreed, giving him just 17 points, but he was kept off the bottom spot by John Sergeant.

Craig Gets Saucy and Gooey

Austin's open-necked samba shirt got everyone in a naughty mood, with Tess running her finger down his chest and Arlene suggesting he had too many muscles for the samba. Craig shocked the other judges when he replied, 'I like the tightness of your upper body – in a dance way, obviously!' Later, Craig declared that Christine's smile made him 'feel all warm and gooey'.

Don's Spirits Dampened

Austin slipped to fourth after Tom and Lisa tied at the top of the table and Rachel lost some of her sparkle in the samba. A disappointed James hit back at Craig's criticism of Cherie's smooth, saying he was 'all quantity and no quality'. And despite middling scores of 23 and 25, the public vote left Don and Heather battling it out in the dance-off, and the *Rising Damp* star took his last bow.

EPISODE 6

Caveman John's Prehistoric Paso

Having survived another round, John Sergeant was back in week six to perform a paso doble from the Ice Age, where he dragged Kristina across the floor as if he had clubbed

her on the head. '*Dad's Army* does the paso!' declared an amused Bruno but the couple still stayed off the bottom of the table with 21.

Cherie's Bullring Blunder

The elegant Ms Lunghi missed her footing at the beginning of her paso doble and paid the price in her score. After Craig pointed out the slip she replied, 'I went completely wrong in the beginning. I own up.' Austin and Erin twirled their way back to the top with a stunning Viennese waltz, which had Bruno gushing, 'It's like watching the return of the king.'

Swimmer Sinks

Jodie and Ian failed to impress with their paso, which Bruno called 'a paso ruffle – it was rough for you and it was rough to watch.' But the worst criticism was directed at Mark Foster, whose Latin was described as 'grotesque' by Craig, while Len philosophized, 'You're no good at dancing. I'm no good at swimming. One of those things.' The eliminated swimmer soon cheered up the ladies by stripping off to show his pecs.

EPISODE 7

Jodie's Full of Pride

In an attempt to bring some romance into their week-seven waltz, Jodie Kidd and Ian Waite turned to Austen (Jane not Healey).

With Ian dressed as Mr Darcy, the pair went riding in the woods before promising 'the most romantic waltz *Strictly* has ever seen'. They charmed three of the judges but Craig decided it was all 'too Mills & Boon for me'.

Wet Weekend

Having scored just three from Craig the week before, Christine was upset when her American smooth to 'Singin' In The Rain' dampened the mood. 'The face was singing in the rain, the legs were crying in a puddle,' said Bruno. Austin was elated after winning the first ten of the series for his waltz to the appropriate track 'It's Wonderful', but Rachel's jive brought more disappointment to Len.

Bouncy-Castle Blues

Samba training proved painful for Andrew, who damaged his cartilage while attempting a knee slide. He battled through but may have wished he hadn't when Len told him, 'Instead of Andrew Castle you should be more of a bouncy castle.' Arlene told him to get out of the 'frozen-food aisle' and into the exotic, and it was game over for the former tennis player.

EPISODE 8

Tess Dancing

Tess had the tables turned on her when Anton revealed their training for a special dance for Children In Need, against Terry Wogan and Flavia Cacace. While practising a lift, Tess smacked her hand on the ceiling and flinched. 'There's only five days to go and I'm dreading it. Any tips, Brucie?' she asked. 'Yes, don't turn up,' he quipped.

Tom Hits a Wall

Tom was very excited about doing the quickstep but training proved harder than he imagined. After banging his elbow on the wall, he said, 'I feel like I've not only hit a physical wall but a mental wall.' But the Fred Astaire fanatic won the judges over, with Len calling the dance 'charming' and Craig announcing it was 'Fab-U-Lous!' Straight to the top of the class with four nines.

Christine Proves Craig Wrong

After the previous week when Arlene told Christine to go to ballet lessons, Craig was forced to eat his words when they succeeded. 'I said last week they wouldn't make any difference and they did!' he admitted. Cherie and Lisa proved a match for Tom, joining him on the top spot with 36 points each for their waltz and their Viennese, while Rachel found herself in her first dance-off. But it was dance-off veteran Heather who finally found the exit.

EPISODE 9

Bad Boy Brendan Erupts

Lisa's salsa aroused passions among the judges and set Brendan aflame! After Craig told her the rolls weren't smooth, Bruno and Len rounded on him. As the row ensued, Brendan lost his temper and banged the judges' table, saying, 'This is about Lisa – come on, boys!'

Lady and the Vamp

Austin fought back from his ropey rumba with a tingling tango that ignited the judges and earned him his highest score of the series with 38. Craig called it 'rugby-licious' and Arlene said it had 'torrid passion'. But, after a night of sharing spaghetti *Lady and the Tramp* style, Rachel and Vincent put just as much raunch into their rumba and stunned the judges into a 39. Bad luck, Austin!

Cherie Pipped at the Post

Jodie and Christine triumphed in the quickstep and waltz but Cherie's cha cha cha, while earning her a score of 32, still landed her in the dance-off with Lisa, who scored 30. The judges lost patience with the public, who once again saved lowest-scorer John, and when Cherie was booted out, a furious James made a plea. 'I would say to the people at home, this is supposed to be a dance contest. Please, please, vote on the dancing.'

EPISODE 10

John Throws in the Towel

Facing a jive, and a whole lot more criticism from the judges, John held a press conference and quit the show. Jeremy Paxman announced, 'A dream died today – John Sergeant has hung up his sequins.' As week ten opened, Len spoke for all the judges when he said, 'We're sorry John has gone because he gave us and the viewers so much entertainment and we wish him well in whatever he does next.'

Camilla Gets Slap Happy

Struggling with the passion of the tango, Camilla took Tom back to the set of *Holby* to recreate a steamy scene between his character and Amanda Mealing's Connie, where she slapped him before kissing him. Camilla enjoyed a little slapping too and, after a turbulent tango, Bruno told him, 'Talk about arrogance! That was disdainful.'

Austin Healey is Clapped Out

After coping with increased training for two dances, and baby twins who were teething, Austin was feeling the strain. Erin told him, 'I need you to get some sleep.' But after a 36 for the foxtrot, a masterful Austin split the judges with his cape action in the paso. Len told him, 'It was all performance and no content,' while Bruno called him 'the lord of the paso!'

Perfect Package

After achieving a record rumba score of 39 the week before, Rachel went one step further with her foxtrot – and landed a perfect score. Bruno called it 'close to heaven' and Arlene '*strictly* something special'. While Christine landed the lowest score, a dance-off between Lisa and Jodie saw the polo-playing model ride off into the sunset.

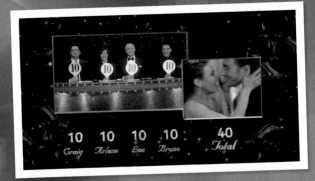

Christine Tastes the Good Life

The One Show presenter got an acting lesson from one of the best when *Strictly* fan Felicity Kendal showed up to help her with her tango. 'If you feel it, people will believe it and that will work,' she advised. Despite a competent performance, things looked bleak for Bleakley when she landed in the dance-off against Rachel and, sure enough, the Irish eyes were smiling all the way home.

EPISODE 11

From Tears to Triumph

The waterworks were flowing in week 11 as Rachel struggled with learning two dances and broke down in training, while Lisa dissolved when talking about the previous week's dance-off, saying, 'It's knocked my confidence.' Even so, Rachel and Vincent scooped a huge 39 for their waltz and a total of 71, while Lisa topped the table with 76 with a cha cha cha and foxtrot.

EPISODE 12

It's Raining Tens

With four couples left in the quarter-finals, it really was anybody's game and it seemed the judges had a hard time choosing between them. Lisa and Brendan were ecstatic after receiving three tens for their first waltz, and a total score of 39, but they were quickly equalled by a foxtrot from Tom and Camilla and a tango from Rachel and Vincent.

Tomcat Turns Kitten

Having received his first ten the week before, Tom admitted, 'It was my best moment so far on *Strictly*.' But after a fantastic foxtrot, the emotional actor was in tears before the judges even gave their verdict. 'Tom, you're an absolute beauty! You came out and knocked my socks off,' said Len. Their rumba split the judges but gave them an overall 73, second on the leader board.

Austin's Final Shootout

In training for the American smooth, Austin quipped, 'This is a dance I've been looking forward to the whole series. There's no point in having muscles if you can't do lifts!' But the dance failed to live up to the stiff competition and his sexy salsa couldn't save him from the dance-off. Austin got the guns out one more time as he pulled off his shirt in the farewell dance.

EPISODE 13

RRRRRRachel Rocks

Vincent wasn't convinced Rachel could handle his speciality Argentine tango: 'It takes two to tango and at the moment I feel I am giving my 50 per cent and Rachel is struggling.' On the night she proved him wrong with a score of 39 and a dance Len called 'a technical *tour de force*'. A dashing American smooth then gained her another 37, leaving her tying with Lisa at the top of the table.

Brendan Blubs

The tables were turned in training as Brendan attempted to tackle the Argentine tango for the first time: 'Lisa is noticing things that I'm doing wrong and putting it right.' After a score of 35, the couple moved on to the quickstep. 'My only complaint last time was the gapping,' said Len. 'This time you were velcroed together. It was Fab-U-Lous!' Both Lisa and Brendan were in tears after their first perfect score.

Unlucky for Some

Tom's jive was 'more exciting than the 50-per-cent-off sale at Woolworths', according to Arlene, but Bruno thought he may have met his Waterloo. After an Argentine tango that scored 34, the couple were left with 67, at the bottom of the leader board. With Camilla in tears at the thought of bowing out in another semi-final, it was revealed that the tie at the top meant the public votes couldn't save the bottom couple, so all three couples went through to the final.

THE FINAL

Lisa's Dream is Over

With four dances to learn for the final, the pressure was on for all three couples. 'Let the battle commence,' challenged Lisa and she put up the best fight of all. After a perfect foxtrot, which Bruno said turned her into 'a creature of almost mythical glamour and technical excellence', they pulled off a cha cha cha that earned another 40, giving them a perfect score of 80 and reducing Brendan to tears, again. Sadly, the public vote had them out first, but Lisa took it well.

Foxy Rachel

Rachel and Vincent matched Lisa's perfect score for a foxtrot, which Len described as 'truly a joy' and Craig as 'absolutely gorgeous'. 'You shimmer and shine like the diamonds on your dress,' said Arlene. After gaining 39 for her rumba, Rachel and Vincent joined Tom and Camilla for the Viennese waltz before a 'scorching' showdance.

What a Show!

Tom slipped at the start of his final foxtrot but went on to perform a sizzling salsa that left Len 'knocked out' and landed a score of 38. At the bottom of the table, it was down to the showdance to make the difference. 'I liked Rachel's but this was something else!' said Len, and all Arlene could say was 'Wow!' Tom clinched the trophy and Camilla retired from the series a winner.

Yet another busy year for head judge Len. With 16 celebrities making the series longer, a Christmas special, two series of *Dancing with the Stars* and a five-week live tour, it's a marvel that he still manages to run his successful dance school in Kent.

But if you thought all the jet-setting and hard work was turning him into a grouch during series six, the down-to-earth dance teacher says you couldn't be more wrong. Like all the judges, Len found series six one of the most exciting so far and, if he appeared grumpy, he has an explanation why:

'My philosophy, by and large, has always been to give positives before giving any negatives. I like to critique my opinion of a dance by saying things like, "Good hold, and your posture was great, unfortunately blah blah blah …" Sometimes, because they say we only have two minutes, you can't embellish so you have to go with the negatives because it would be ludicrous to say, "I thought that was absolutely fantastic, you danced that brilliantly," then give them an eight.

'A live show has to finish on time, and the dances all have to be 90 seconds so it's very difficult to gain or lose time other than through the judges,' he explains.

'Quite often, while viewers are watching the training video, the producer will come over and say, "We're two minutes over time; please keep your comments to five seconds."

'Last year a lot of people said I was a bit grumpy but I was just being concise! For whatever reason, we always

seemed to be running a bit over time, so we had to be very brief.'

'That's why I thought it was good that the audience got to see our backstage discussions for the first time last year. All those things help to give the viewers a bit of an insight into how the judges are thinking.'

Last series proved to be a very different end game from previous years, and Len was delighted that there were so many contenders for the title. The viewers had no idea who was going to cross the finish line and Len's tip for the top fell earlier than expected.

'There was no clear front runner and that's what made this series so great,' he says. 'Right up until virtually the end I had the feeling that Austin Healey was going to win. In the quarter-finals the two girls and the two boys were equally strong and once he got knocked out it did become absolutely open for any of the other three couples. It was amazing.'

The series was not without its controversies, however, and Len was as surprised as the other judges when the audience vote was suspended in the semi-final because of the tie at the top of the judges' leader board.

'In a ballroom or Latin competition, you cannot let anyone tie,' he explains. 'If there are four couples in a final you have to mark them first, second, third, fourth, so you have a clear winner from each of the judges. On *Strictly*, it's difficult to do that because if one couple dances and you give them a seven, the next one comes out and he's better, so you give him an eight. Then the third one comes out and they're better than the one who got a seven but not as good as the one who got an eight, so what do you do?' Luckily, this year the new voting system should prevent hitches like this happening again.

Being the oldest on the panel, Len has a reputation for sticking up for the more senior celebrities on the show. And, despite telling John Sergeant 'It's not Help The Aged', he was supportive of the flat-footed broadcaster in his own inimitable way.

'One week, when he did get a bit of stick, including from me, I said, "If I was at home, voting, I would bring you back, John," because he was entertaining, you never knew what you were going to get and it's all part of the charm of the show.

'I'm glad I said that because the judges came in for a lot of criticism from the press, who were saying it's an entertainment as well as a dance show, which I agree with, but we are employed to critique the dancing.

'As I've said many times in the past, the viewers can judge with their hearts but the judges have to judge with their brains, and judge the dancing alone. What makes the show so great is that the viewers can say, "Sod the judges. He's good fun and we want to see him again next week." Good luck to them.'

He was disappointed, however, when the veteran journalist left the show early.

'I think it was a mistake that he gave up and he gave the reason that there was a possibility he could win. Well, my opinion is that the British love an underdog; we always have. But above that we believe in justice and there does come a point where justice will prevail.

'If he'd been going along and had knocked Rachel or Tom out, then people would have said, "This is ludicrous," and voted the other way. Then he'd have been kicked off.'

Familiarity, they say, breeds contempt and on screen the judges seemed to be at each other's throats more often than usual in series six. Even in week one, Len castigated the other three as 'deplorable' after they were less than complimentary about Don Warrington, and he told Craig 'You get on my wick!' on several occasions. Off screen, however, it was all sweetness and light.

'We all get on great backstage, despite our rows,' he reveals. 'We always have our little flare ups but they don't transfer after the show. Once the show's over that's that. But the beauty of our different backgrounds is that we have a balanced view. Take Austin Healey's paso, which the other three loved but I thought lacked content. I might not agree but I can understand the viewers and the other judges being swept away with the performance level of it, which was brilliant.

'The week before the final, we have always gone off somewhere and had dinner together, and they are a really nice group of people.

'I have a lot of respect for Craig. And Bruno and I get on really well as we fly back and forth to the States together all the time. I will miss Arlene not being on the judges panel this year but I look forward to welcoming Alesha. I always got on very well with Arlene and I have a great respect for her as a choreographer – she's probably THE leading choreographer in the UK if not the world.'

Ali Bastian
Brian Fortuna

Fans of *The Bill* are more used to seeing Ali in regulation black flats than crystal-coated heels, and the talented actress is looking forward to swapping her uniform for something a bit more glamorous.

'I have watched *Strictly Come Dancing* for the last few years and have always wanted to take part,' she reveals. 'I know it's probably a girly cliché but I just can't wait to wear all the beautiful dresses – it'll be fantastic. The girly fantasy aside, it will of course be great to learn the new dances.'

The 27 year old from Windsor, who has been acting from the age of ten, shot to fame as teacher Becca Dean in *Hollyoaks* and met a nasty end in prison after having a fling with one of her students. Switching from convict to copper, she joined the cast of *The Bill* as Sally Armstrong, a passionate WPC who often pushes the boundaries in order to solve a case.

Fitness shouldn't be a problem if her 2005 DVD *Hollyoaks Get Fit* is anything to go by, and dancing should be in her blood too. Her grandmother competed in ballroom and even gave Ali a few lessons.

'I've done bits and pieces of dancing before,' she says. 'When I was younger my gran tried to teach me how to do the foxtrot. But after drama school I followed acting rather than dancing.'

And she has already been trying to get a head start on the other contestants.

'Ever since I found out about *Strictly* I have been in a panic. I have been at the gym doing salsa aerobics or any class that involves some kind of dance, which I know is just a workout class but I have tried anything that might help.'

At 5' 8" the star is just the right height for both Latin and ballroom, and is keen to try her hand at both.

'I love to watch the Latin, but at the same time I enjoy the ballroom. I think I love it all!' she laughs. 'The Latin looks really challenging, especially the samba, which looks very tricky, so I am looking forward to that. Ballroom is a bit more daunting as I can struggle with posture so we shall see.'

She is unfazed by the ordeal of facing the judges because she believes their barbed comments are all in the best interest of the dancer.

'Whenever I have watched *Strictly Come Dancing* in the past I have always found the criticism very constructive – those judges really know what they are talking about.

'I hope I'll be able to listen to the criticism and then go away and work harder. I think I'm going to have to grow some very thick skin before the first live show though.'

A long-term fan of the show, Ali can't wait to start dancing with American professional Brian Fortuna.

'When I got the call from *Strictly Come Dancing* I was beside myself and I still am!' she gushes. 'I feel like this is an experience that will stay with me for the rest of my life. It's going to be a lot of hard work but I can't wait to get stuck in.'

She does have one fear as she embarks on her dancing journey, however.

'I'm scared of falling down the steps on the show!'

Brian Fortuna

American boy Brian was one of three new dancers in the last series and was teamed with M People diva Heather Small. The couple made it to week eight.

Brian grew up in Philadelphia, where he was taught to dance by his mother, professional dancer Sandra Fortuna, and the world-renowned Corky Ballas. At five, Brian was already competing and as a teenager he began to teach at his mother's dance school, Universal.

Brian specialises in wheelchair ballroom and Latin dancing and in 2004 he was voted North American Top Teacher. The 27 year old competed in *Dancing with the Stars* in the US before joining the UK *SCD* family.

Favourite dance?
The jive because it's fast, fun and emanates from the world of rock and roll. Foxtrot is my favourite ballroom dance, mainly thanks to Frank Sinatra.

How was your *Strictly* debut?
Dancing with Heather was great fun. There was never a moment without a laugh. Everyone on the show is great – some of the most fun people I have ever been around.

Approach to teaching?
I think a celebrity needs to learn to dance just like anyone else by committing to hard work and sacrifice. But it's a blast to introduce a celebrated artist to the magic of dance. It changes their life for ever.

Ideal celeb?
I want to dance with someone who is fun to work with, has a positive attitude, and is excited to learn the new dances. I trust I will be matched up with the perfect celebrity. Working with someone who has a background in professional sports is ideal because they know what it takes to train to be the best at something. Ideally, I want Tess Daly to give up her job as host of the show and come dance with me.

What have you been doing since last year?
I went home to visit my family, and toured the UK in shows with Kristina Rihanoff. I have also been working as a choreographer and producer on *Dancing on Wheels*, a new series for BBC Three featuring wheelchair dancing, which my mother also took part in. It's a subject close to both of our hearts as both of us have taught it for several years. The show brings disabled and able-bodied people to dance together so it will really be something special.

Hopes for series seven?
I'd like a partner I get along with very well and that I enjoy spending time with. And I am looking forward to some more exciting professional dances with my *Strictly* partner Kristina.

Alesha Unleashed

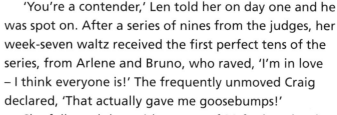

For series seven, Alesha Dixon makes the crossover from judged to judge as she joins Len Goodman, Bruno Tonioli and Craig Revel Horwood on the panel.

'I am so excited about being a judge on *Strictly*,' she says. 'I absolutely loved competing on the programme and so now to be a judge is just so fantastic. The best thing about being a judge is the fact I will have the best seat in the house.

'I didn't have to think twice when I was asked. I love a new challenge.'

Two years ago the talented singer realised a lifelong dream when she twirled her way to triumph with professional partner Matthew Cutler. As a child growing up in Welwyn Garden City, she had been forced to give up ballet and tap lessons when her single mum could no longer afford them and, instead, made up routines with her friends in the playground.

Discovered in a dance studio in Fulham as a teenager, Alesha forged a successful career with garage and R&B band Mis-Teeq, releasing two platinum-selling albums and numerous top-ten hits, including 'Scandalous' and 'All I Want'. The band split in 2005 after their record company folded, and Alesha married So Solid Crew member MC Harvey and embarked on a solo career.

A year later both were cruelly snatched from her when her label dropped her before the album was released, and Harvey's affair with West End co-star Javine Hylton was revealed in the papers.

Strictly Come Dancing marked a turning point in the stunning star's fortune. A natural at the Latin dances, she astounded the viewers and the judges with her elegant ballroom too.

'You're a contender,' Len told her on day one and he was spot on. After a series of nines from the judges, her week-seven waltz received the first perfect tens of the series, from Arlene and Bruno, who raved, 'I'm in love – I think everyone is!' The frequently unmoved Craig declared, 'That actually gave me goosebumps!'

She followed that with a score of 39 for her cha cha cha and by the quarter-finals she had already collected more tens than any other contestant so far. 'I never want to stop watching her dance,' said Arlene.

A thrilling final saw her pitted against dashing *EastEnders* actor Matt Di Angelo – but it was Alesha and Matthew who finally picked up the glitter-ball trophy.

'She does class and she does sexy,' said Bruno. 'She does beauty and she does beast. What more do you want?'

In 12 months, Alesha's life had turned around and Christmas 2007 was the start of a new era.

'I thought 2007 was going to be terrible, but because of *Strictly* my confidence is back,' she said, after winning the trophy. 'Dancing saved me. I've got the real me back. This is the best Christmas present ever.'

With her solo career back on track after hit records 'The Boy Does Nothing' and 'Breathe Slow', Alesha is ready for a new challenge and is hoping she'll be a hit as a judge. And she believes her own experiences on the show will allow her to approach the dances from a different angle.

'I'd like to think I will be a very honest judge. If I like something, then the celebrities will know about it. If I don't I will try to be constructive,' she says. 'I have got great empathy with the celebrities taking part. I know exactly how they are feeling and all the different emotions they will go through at every stage of the *Strictly* competition.'

Presenter Tess Daly is looking forward to having her long-time pal on the show. 'I've always been a huge champion of Alesha's, ever since I first met her back in 2001 on *SM: TV*, and she was in Mis-Teeq,' she reveals. 'She co-hosted a couple of the shows with myself and Brian Dowling and I've been a fan since then. I think she's hugely talented and a drop-dead beauty and I think she'll be a very welcome addition to the show.

'She'll bring that sparkly effervescence and I think she will keep the judges in order. She'll be a rose among thorns.'

And the blooming beauty is thrilled to be seated alongside the spiky stars.

'I really liked all the other judges when I competed and I can't wait to work alongside them on the new series,' she gushes. 'I am sure there will be plenty of banter between us all because it is impossible for four people to agree – but *Strictly* is an entertainment show and the banter is part of the fun. I am very open-minded to people's opinions.

'I hope the celebrities taking part will go on the show with a drive to enjoy learning to dance and go into it with passion. *Strictly* is a once-in-a-lifetime experience and it is so much fun.'

Darcey Drops In

This year the judging panel will benefit from the considerable experience of Darcey Bussell.

Britain's best-known prima ballerina, Darcey has been dancing since the age of 13 and joined The Royal Ballet in 1988 after her talent was spotted by choreographer Kenneth MacMillan. At 20, on the opening night of her first major show, *The Prince of the Pagodas,* she was promoted to become the company's youngest-ever principal dancer.

She retired from ballet in 2007, with a farewell performance in MacMillan's *Song of the Earth* at the Royal Opera House, which earned her a standing ovation of over eight minutes.

The 40-year-old now lives in Sydney with her husband and two children, and is a director of the Sydney Dance Company. She will serve as guest judge on the *Strictly* panel as the competition hots up in the run-up to the final.

'Darcey has impeccable credentials as a dancer and as a guest judge,' said BBC1 controller Jay Hunt. 'She will bring an exciting new dimension to the last few weeks of the *Strictly* competition.'

A fan of the show, the elegant star is excited to be joining the judges for series seven.

'It is a real pleasure to have been invited to join *Strictly Come Dancing*,' she says. 'It is a fantastic show and I'm looking forward to getting to know the dancers and being part of the excitement.'

Lynda Bellingham
Darren Bennett

Lynda may be the oldest competitor in this year's show but she is determined to show the younger celebs a thing or two.

'I may well be the elderly statesperson on the show, which I would be more than happy with,' she declares. 'I would relish the opportunity to show those doubters out there, of which I'm sure there are many, that life does not end at 40!'

Lynda's 40-year career has made her a national treasure, with roles in *At Home with the Braithwaites*, *All Creatures Great and Small* and *Within These Walls.* One of her most memorable roles was, of course, playing the world-famous Oxo mum. It was a 16-year stint in which 42 different commercials were made for the Oxo series, and they are still often voted the country's most popular ads.

Judges who have watched her latest incarnation, as a straight-talking panellist on popular daytime show *Loose Women*, may be reluctant to criticise for fear of what she might say back! But Lynda doesn't think their comments will bother her too much.

'I have faced rejection from various casting directors over the years so I should be OK with someone being mean about my footwork,' she reckons. 'Craig can be quite cutting, though. I'd like to think that I could offer a witty riposte if he was ever over the top.'
Despite the potential criticism, she is delighted to be on the show.

'I, along with pretty much the whole of the country, think *Strictly Come Dancing* is absolutely fantastic and was absolutely thrilled when I was asked to be involved,' she reveals. '*Strictly* is the only show of its kind in which the participants are able to learn a new skill. I know the judges can sometimes be cutting with their remarks but there's no cruelty to the programme. Don't get me wrong, I'm prepared to have the proverbial taken out of me on the show, especially if I mess things up on the night. I'll be the first to laugh at myself, in fact!

'The show as a whole is good family entertainment and I'm totally honoured to have been asked.'

The 61-year-old star, who trained at the Central School of Speech and Drama in London, has crossed paths with presenter Bruce Forsyth before and is looking forward to seeing him again.

'I actually remember seeing him sometime in the 70s when I was in New York,' she recalls. 'He had a one-man show on Broadway and I was lucky enough to get a ticket. In those days it was

a real achievement for a Brit to have a show on Broadway and he was absolutely fantastic. He had Sammy Davis Jr on as a guest, I remember.

'After the show I was smuggled into his dressing room to say hello and to offer my congratulations on how his show had gone.'

The bubbly actress hasn't always been so keen to learn to dance. Lynda attended dance classes for a short while in her teens, to begin with against her will, but doesn't think this experience will give her any real advantage over the other contestants.

'My mum made me attend ballroom classes when I was in my early teens,' she admits. 'I didn't want to go at first but became very attached to both the course and my teacher. I hope some of the education from those classes will have stayed with me but that experience was many moons ago though so it's unlikely!

'I remember some of the dancing lingo but the club never ran any competitions, so who knows how good I really was.

Apart from the training, Lynda has already been through the mill trying to keep her participation in the show from her friends and family.

'It's been hard keeping it a secret. It's a big relief to me because as an actor you spend half your life pretending that you've got a job to go to and you haven't, so when you've got a job and you can't tell anyone, it's tough.'

In fact, at the time of interview she hadn't even told her sons, Michael, 26, and Robbie, 21.

'At the moment my sons have no idea that I'm involved. I think they'll be horrified when they discover what's going on! Embarrassing mum and all that!'

Those family members she has told, including her husband Michael, are supportive – if not necessarily for the right reasons.

'My sister is such a huge fan and would never forgive me for turning down this opportunity,' she says.

'My biggest regret is that my parents are no longer around to see me take part. They would have viewed this as the pinnacle of my career.

'My husband is thrilled that I'm involved as he hopes I'll lose some weight. Charming, eh?!'

Darren Bennett

Latin champ Darren grew up around dance. His mother and father are professionals and own a dance school in his native Sheffield, and twin brother Dale is also on the circuit. In fact, it was Dale who introduced Darren to Russian minx Lilia, whom he took on as his partner after a 15-minute trial and married 18 months later.

Darren made his *Strictly* debut in series two, where he jived his way to victory with ex-*EastEnder* Jill Halfpenny. Since then he has dropped out in week four with both Gloria Hunniford and Jessie Wallace, made it to the semis with Emma Bunton and the quarter-finals with Letitia Dean.

How did you get on with your celeb partners?

Jill was really keen and turned into a truly talented dancer, so she was a joy. Emma was fantastic. She was such a high-profile celebrity yet she was so easy to work with. We both had such a great time on the show; she always worked so hard in training.

Series five was a real rollercoaster of a series because you never knew what was going to happen next. That made it one of the most enjoyable yet. In series six I saw the potential in Jessie, not just as a dancer but as a person. It's a shame she didn't stay in the competition longer so the audience could see the real Jessie.

How does it feel to leave early?

It's not about the winning but not being able to perform and showcase yourself as a dancer is very hard. But I was proud of Lilia winning in series three. If I can't win, I would love my wife to do it instead!

What have you done since the last series?

The great thing this year has been doing the Live Tour. Dancing with Jill Halfpenny again and working with the other celebrities and pros on a daily basis has been great.

Lilia and I have also choreographed *Latin Fever* and have fronted a campaign to introduce dancing into schools.

There's massive enthusiasm for dancing and that doesn't diminish through the year, but everyone is looking forward to the show coming back – they're all dying to see it and waiting with anticipation.

Ideal celeb?

Kylie Minogue – it's a height thing!

I'd like someone who has the same drive as me, someone with a positive mental attitude to come to training, perform in the show and have determination to do their very best.

Favourite dance?

The Samba - I love the different types of music and rhythms you can play with. It's a really creative dance.

Hopes for series seven?

To go as far as I possibly can so that I can choreograph and be part of the show and explore all the opportunities with my new dance partner

Every year is so different, two partners are never the same, so it's a new challenge each year, which I relish. After six series, I'm always thinking what new and exciting things we can bring to the show to make it bigger and better.

Bruno Reports Back

Bruno Tonioli is looking forward to the next series and seeing the latest batch of willing celebrities strut their stuff.

But he reveals he never indulges in preconceptions about how well they will dance.

'Until I see the celebs actually perform it's all pie in the sky,' he says. 'You have to see them dance and then, after the first couple of weeks, you can start to make up your mind a little bit more.'

Last year the effusive Italian had high praise for 'Rrrrrrrrachel' and in the semi-final, although Tom danced well, he was outshone by the girls who thrilled him with the standard of their performances.

'It was a case of Girl Power unleashed because both my girls did me proud,' he said. 'Lisa's quickstep was worthy of a ballroom star. Rachel's Argentine tango, which is technically so difficult, she did with the assurance of a professional and to do that is hard.'

And he maintains that she was the best dancer in the competition, despite her defeat in the final.

'I always thought that Rachel was the best but it often happens that the final dance can swing it.

'We had the same thing in America, where I judge *Dancing with the Stars.* One couple slightly misjudged the freestyle. Tom's freestyle was fantastic and the rules of the contest are that you judge on what you see and in the final that clinched Tom the title.

'Rachel was a consistent dancer and absolutely wonderful, but when I am on the show I have to do my job, which is to comment on what I see. Tom's showdance was better and that really lost Rachel the vote.

'As I said at the time, showdances could never be more showy than that one – from Hollywood to Broadway and back again.

'That's what's so amazing about the show – you have to keep your eye on the ball all the way through.

'The final show is like the final of Wimbledon: it doesn't matter what you did to get there, you can't afford to drop the ball.'

Most Improved

Lisa, with no hesitation. She was incredible. At the start she was gangly and goofy, and she turned out to be a stunner. As I said in the final, she turned into a creature of almost mythical glamour and she danced like a dream.

Shock Exit

Cherie Lunghi went out too early. She was class. So lovely. She had a fair go at the Latin and she danced absolutely beautiful ballroom — such a leading lady.

Biggest Surprise

Austin was a lot better than I thought he'd be and he really got the girls going. He was our own little version of Cristiano Ronaldo! His first waltz was a revelation. He's a big bruiser of a man and he was so light on his feet, so elegant.

Most Memorable Dance

Rachel's rumba stood out for me. It was one of the best rumbas ever. Rumbas are rarely executed to such a level of intensity and passion and Len thought it was a little bit TOO raunchy but he's an old fuddy-duddy. For any young, hot-blooded male, I tell you, that rumba is better than Viagra!

Worst Dancer

Gary Rhodes — a master in the kitchen, a disaster on the dance floor.

On Christine's American smooth to 'Singin' In The Rain':
'The face was singing in the rain, the legs were crying in a puddle.'

On John Sergeant's samba:
'Maybe for hip action you need a hip replacement!'

On Jodie's rumba:
'You remind me of a classic Maserati. Curves all over the place, great to look at, but you keep stalling.'

On Mark's paso doble:
'You look like a god; you dance like a geek!'

On Rachel's paso doble:
'We had the angel, now we have the devil! Senorita Rachel, you can have any bull you want – you can have mine!'

On Austin Healey's salsa:
'I tell you, this performance will get you the pink pound!'

On Lisa's Argentine tango:
'The first thing I saw was Lisa's legs reaching to the outer limit. You were wrapping around Brendan like Octopussy.'

On Rachel's final rumba:
'Rachel, I need a shower, a stiff drink, then let's do it all over again! Not only seductive, it was addictive!'

Joe Calzaghe CBE, MBE
Kristina Rihanoff

As he's used to dancing round the ring, boxer Joe should prove light on his feet. So will he be a knockout on the dance floor?

'I'm nervous about little things like treading on my partner's toes or forgetting the routine,' he admits. 'I'm very scared about dancing in front of a live audience. I know it may not seem obvious but I am quite a shy guy. I am happy boxing in the ring in front of thousands of people, but the thought of dancing in front of an audience is terrifying.'

The Welsh-born fighter is Britain's only undefeated world champion and the longest reigning champ of the modern era, having held the World Boxing Organisation super-middleweight title for over ten years until he relinquished the title to concentrate on fighting at light heavyweight.

Joe first stepped into the ring at the age of nine and went on to win in the British Schoolboy Championships. Trained by his Sardinian father, Enzo, he turned professional in 1993, making his debut at the Cardiff Arms Park in a support bout before a Frank Bruno fight. Over the next two years, he claimed victory in nine out of nine fights, and was honoured with a Young Boxer of the Year award from the Professional Boxing Association.

The 2007 BBC Sports Personality of the Year and already a Member of the Order of the British Empire (MBE), he was appointed Commander of the Order of the British Empire (CBE) in the 2008 Queen's Birthday Honours. He retired in 2009, with a record 46 professional fights under his many belts, and was awarded the Freedom of Caerphilly.

The competitive spirit that spurs on the *Strictly* stars every year is exactly what got Joe to where he is and is still there in abundance.

'Yes, there have been some hard times, but I've kept plugging away,' he says. 'I was never going to be a nine-to-five man or work shifts in a cake factory, like my mum. I tried it once for a couple of days, sticking stickers on things, but I thought, Screw this for a lark, I want to be a world champion.'

Although no longer boxing, Joe keeps up the fitness regime in the local gym at Newbridge, where he has always trained.

'When nothing's broke, don't try to fix it. Where I live is nice and quiet. I get left alone.

There are beautiful mountains, and every time I run in the morning there's a big hill to climb,' he says. 'I'm happy sticking to the same routine and that's probably why I've had this tremendous consistency and fitness. I've been training nearly every day since I was 13. Even then I had a burning ambition to be a champion.'

Fitness is one reason he signed up to *Strictly*, as well as achieving another first in his chosen sport.

'I agreed to take part in *Strictly Come Dancing* because it is a totally new challenge for me,' says Joe, who is dancing with Kristina Rihanoff.

'Watching the show in the past, I have noticed how hard the celebrities have to train in order to reach the standards they attain on a Saturday night. I wanted to take part because I am a competitor, I like to keep in shape and the show has a good history of sportsmen doing well. I am proud to represent the fighter on the show and become the first boxer to take part in *Strictly Come Dancing*!'

And he is keen to keep up the standard displayed by sportsmen such as Mark Ramprakash, Colin Jackson, Matt Dawson and Darren Gough.

'Of all the series of *Strictly Come Dancing*, there is one performance that stands head and shoulders above the rest and that is Darren Gough's,' he says. 'He showed remarkable skill on the dance floor. I'd like to maintain the good reputation that sportsmen have developed on the show.'

While you might think the sequined shirts and diamanté shoes would put a macho fighter such as Joe off the dancing, he is actually looking forward to the glitzy costumes.

'Ballroom dancing looks easier than the Latin to me but to be honest I prefer the look and costumes involved in Latin,' he admits. 'Throughout my boxing career I always wore shiny black sequins on my boxing shorts, so I'm no stranger to a bit of sparkle.'

Kristina Rihanoff

Last year, Siberian stunner Kristina made a memorable debut on *Strictly* partnering the clumsy but comic John Sergeant. Since then she has partnered Matthew Cutler on the *SCD* tour and taken part in a TV show with Brian Fortuna that aims to bring dance to the disabled.

Kristina started dancing at the age of six, becoming a National Champion before she was 16. In 2001 she was invited to compete in the United States and moved to Seattle. Three years later she was representing her adopted country in the World Exhibition at the Blackpool Dance Festival.

Favourite dance?

I love the rumba. That is the woman's dance. As it is so slow, it allows the lady to be very sensual and beautiful. The rumba really shows off the leg action and footwork. In ballroom, I would choose the waltz – I think it is the most graceful and romantic. It reminds me of an evening at the palace with the royal family when all the ladies look like princesses.

What's the secret to teaching celebs?

The main thing is to understand the other person's way of learning. I have been teaching a lot of beginners and you need to find a way to make it simple for them while having fun and finding cool ways to explain things. Then, even when the work gets hard, they still feel like they are having a good time and accomplishing something great.

Respect, of course, is also the key to a successful working relationship. No matter what, both people have to be respectful of each other and never use negative words or behave rudely.

Ideal celeb?

I would love to work with an athlete because they are very good with instruction. They know how to be taught and follow their teacher, and that's why they are so successful. But you also need someone with a good personality. I hope I'll have someone with audience appeal and chemistry. Above all, I'd like a great character with an open mind – someone who wants to win, but will have fun on the journey.

What did you make of John Sergeant?

I didn't know what to expect for my first year on the series. It was the biggest surprise of my professional career to be partnered by John Sergeant. When I saw him I thought, Oh my God, what am I going to do?

But I learned *Strictly Come Dancing* is not only about dancing but also popularity. John was really popular and knew how to connect with the public. Working with him was the perfect combination of popularity and ability. He was kind and respectful – you can't wish for anything better. The audience saw that we had respect for each other and how much we enjoyed working together. He was my ideal partner for my first series.

Hopes for series seven?

I hope that the public will be able to connect with my celebrity. I want to take my partner all the way to the final this time. I am a skilful teacher and if I have someone good next to me I know we can make it.

Natalie Cassidy
& Vincent Simone

Natalie follows many former residents of Albert Square in swapping the Queen Vic for the quickstep. Although she is only 26, the talented actress has been in the public eye from a young age, having made her *EastEnders* debut at the age of ten as the young Sonia Jackson.

She has often been in the audience to support her co-stars, including Matt Di Angelo, Jill Halfpenny and Gillian Taylforth.

'It's my favourite show,' she admits. 'I've watched *Strictly* every single year since the show started. I've been in the audience dozens of times supporting Jill, Matt and Louisa [Lytton] over the years. I have had so much fun watching them and they look like they have so much fun themselves. The chance to take part was just too irresistible to turn down.

'*Strictly* always reminds me of those great old-fashioned family-entertainment shows such as *The Generation Game* or *Blind Date*. Funny and warm, not crude in any way.

'I love television and I love the theatre and *Strictly* seems the perfect marriage of both. I love Bruce and Tess. I've met Tess and Vernon a few times in the past and they're my favourite celebrity couple.'

Her only regret is that her mum, who she lost to bowel cancer seven years ago, is not there to see her and that Wendy Richard, her 'second mum', sadly passed away earlier this year.

'I just wish my mum could be around to watch me dance,' she says. 'She passed away when I was 19, the year that *Strictly* started. She never was able to watch the show but she would have absolutely loved me being part of all this.'

Despite her support for her fellow *EastEnders*, Natalie admits to a slight disloyalty in series five.

'The year of Alesha was when I was completely hooked,' she recalls. 'I was desperate for Matt to win but Alesha was fantastic and deserved that crown. Matt will kill me for saying that! Alesha was magical. I still watch that final dance on the internet. It was the best piece of television.

'The year before was the year of Ramps. He and Karen were just superb. He was the hipmaster! Incredible stuff. Louisa's jive was wonderful too. I always think of her whenever that Gnarls Barkley song is played.'

The Londoner, who quit *EastEnders* in 2007, is looking forward to bonding with her fellow contestants.

'I'm hoping this will be the best experience ever,' she says. 'Everybody always looks like one big, happy family and I so hope this is the case this year. I hope I make dozens of lovely friends and win!'

Judging by her preferred music, Natalie, who will dance with Vincent Simone, may well be more of a ballroom belle than a Latin lover.

'I'm always the first up on the dance floor on a night out or at a do,' she reveals. 'At the moment I love that 1950s big-band sound. Sinatra, Dean Martin … Those Rat Pack guys. I have a CD full of songs from that era, which I put on first thing in the morning for a boogie. Hopefully I'm getting some practice in early by doing that.'

And the costumes seem more up her street too.

'The ballroom is magical. Those dresses give the dances a fairytale feel and that's something to look forward to,' she says, smiling.

'I think I would look forward to the Latin dances though. Especially the jive. I'll have a lot of fun with that one.'

Natalie's hoping the judges will be on her side, especially Bruno, who she knows pretty well already. 'I was a judge on *Making Your Mind Up* a couple of years ago and he was too so I actually have some familiarity with being on the other side of the panel,' she remembers. 'I'm an easy-going person. I get on with people and so if the judges do say one or two miserable things then I should be able to handle myself. I'm sure the judges will be professional and constructive and when they are not then I hope the audience voice their disapproval anyway. They're on my side – I hope!'

Vincent Simone

Fiery Italian Vincent is an Argentine tango champion and he certainly got lucky with his celebrity partner in series six. Rachel Stevens' tingling tango left the audience and judges in awe and the couple narrowly missed out on the trophy, thanks to Tom Chambers' showdance.

Vincent has been dancing with Flavia Cacace for 13 years and turned professional in 2001. They joined the show in series four and Vincent made an instant impression by tangoing his way into the quarter-finals with *EastEnder* Louisa Lytton.

When did you start dancing?

All my family are dancers, and my parents are teachers in ballroom and Latin, so my career in dance was bound to happen as dancing is such a massive part of Italian life. I remember that I would dance at any party that we went to. Aged five I would be the one on the dance floor dancing around – my mother said I was born to perform!

What was your first series like for you?

My first time on *SCD* I was extremely lucky to be paired up with Louisa as she was probably one of the most talented celebrities ever to have taken part in *SCD*. We had so much fun during the training sessions as I believe that having fun is the best way to learn to dance! She surprised me every Saturday with her performance, always giving it 100 per cent. She was incredibly bubbly and fun to work with.

How did you get on with Rachel?

Rachel was a dream come true for any dancer. She was a true professional in every way and so inspiring so I couldn't have been happier.

Favourite dance?

The tango, of course. Being the strongest of the ballroom dances, I find the music gives me so much energy. In Latin I love the rumba, as it's the dance of love – romantic, sensual and full of 'passione' – and there's a wider choice of beautiful songs to dance to.

What do you look for in celeb partners?

This year I hope to get someone who is very enthusiastic about the show and learning to dance, with star qualities that will inspire me. And hopefully we'll have a magic connection that will get us to the top.

How has *Strictly* changed your life?

The best part for me when we're not on *Strictly* is to be able to meet and speak to the audience who love the show. I love to see the smiles on people's faces and I love it when many times they tell me meeting me was the best moment of their lives.

The Winner's Story
Doctor of

H olby heartthrob Tom Chambers swapped his hospital gown for a green satin shirt and kicked off series six with a cha cha cha that instantly split the judges.

While Bruno thought he had 'the confidence of a tomcat claiming his new territory', and added, 'I bet there's a few kittens purring around here,' Craig called the dance 'mincey' and 'a tad smug'. The philosophical actor, however, was 'just glad the trousers didn't split'.

Clothing intact, he and partner Camilla Dallerup walked away with the respectable score of 28, losing out only to Austin Healey, whose debut waltz landed him a massive 32.

It was the start of an adventure that Tom had long dreamed of.

'I've always been a huge fan of Fred Astaire and Gene Kelly and I love the musical films from the 1930s, so it's been my ambition to try and bring some of that beautiful stuff back into current entertainment.

'*Strictly* was like a no-brainer for me because being asked to be part of the show and receive one-to-one dance tuition from a first-class professional was like being offered football training from David Beckham.

'To me, going on the show was a bit like getting all you ever wanted as a kid.'

Tom proved so dedicated to the cause that he moved his wedding back a day to take part and postponed his honeymoon until after the series, all with the blessing of bride-to-be Clare.

'It wasn't easy,' he admits. 'You only get married once and our wedding day was the most special thing ever, it really was, but we were lucky because we'd done so much preparation before the show started, which made it less of a problem to move it to the Sunday.

'The hardest part was doing without the honeymoon because we had the Monday after the wedding together and then Camilla and I started

Dance

'Camilla was an iron lady,' he reveals.

'She and Margaret Thatcher could have been related because she's a very hard taskmaster and won't settle for anything but the best.

'We had five months of constant training, every day, for hours and hours, and the pressure on her was greater than on me because she has to teach someone who has never danced this way before; so she would crack the whip. But she also had a great sense of humour and was a lot of fun to work with. She brought a character and charisma to the dance routines.

'She was brilliant but it definitely wasn't a softly, softly approach.'

With his penchant for old Hollywood musicals, Tom naturally gravitated towards the ballroom dances and especially the American smooth. And despite the gleeful declaration from Arlene that 'there is magic in those hips' in week one, it took a while for him to become a lover of Latin.

'The Latin makes blokes cringe a bit because there's a lot of shaking and bum wiggling and it feels a bit more feminine,' he says. 'But we shouldn't feel that way because a true Latin dancer is very masculine and can make it very sexy.

'Before the show I watched previous contestants and tried to see who made it look good. Gethin Jones and Mark Ramprakash were so good at the salsa it helped to watch them and I could see how to put a character on it, add a cheeky smile, tease the audience a little, like you're doing a mating dance.'

On the long road to the final, there were many emotional peaks for Tom but there were one or two troughs as well.

'I was gutted when Austin went out in the quarter-finals because he and I had stayed in while the men were dropping like flies, so it became boys against girls. After he left, it became even more of a fight to

training again on Tuesday. I really wanted to wallow in the fact that I'd waited so long to marry this girl – 11 years – so that was tough.

'Clare was amazingly supportive and brilliant throughout the whole thing but I know she couldn't wait for a little "us" time and being able to go away together, which we did after the series ended.'

As dishy doctor Sam Strachan, Tom is used to steely women melting as soon as he turns on the charm but dance partner Camilla is made of sterner stuff.

stay in it because it left two girls against one boy.

'But the low point for me was when the flaw in the voting system was revealed in the semi-finals because the confusion took away a little bit of the magic of getting through. Some people thought I wouldn't have got through but on a normal evening I would have done because Camilla and I got the highest public vote and so would have been saved from the dance-off.'

Once through to the final, Tom faced stiff competition from Rachel Stevens and Lisa Snowdon, who had been picking up tens and breaking records for weeks.

'The girls both danced like absolute dreams and I felt I was chasing up the rear. The final was a white-knuckle ride because we stumbled in what was otherwise going to be a perfect foxtrot. You could actually hear a sharp intake of breath from the audience and I could just imagine my family at home shouting at the telly, "What have you done?!"'

But, as Bruno pointed out, the viewers were in for a treat as Tom had, 'Like Bisto gravy – saved the best 'til last.' Despite perfect scores for Lisa Snowdon and Rachel Stevens, Tom's triumphant showdance clinched the title.

'Right from the beginning the showdance was the one I couldn't wait for because I didn't much enjoy the judging!' he says. 'I felt the judges were often against me but with the final dance I knew they didn't score so I could entertain the public, who might look at it with a less critical eye and judge with the heart and soul.

'Camilla let me do a few steps on my own at the top, to bring a little bit of story into it, and we made the style more suitable to myself, with a little bit of Fred and Gene.

'We were the first dance of the series and the very last dance as well, which was wonderful and felt like we were closing the circle.'

Finally, after five months of toil, tears and triumph, Tom and Camilla raised the mirrorball trophy and

planted a kiss on its glittering surface.

'It was totally surreal because by the time you are in the final, your head is swimming with so many thoughts that it passes in a bit of a blur. You stand there waiting and when they say your name the whole achievement of getting there comes flooding back.

'But winning the trophy was more about Camilla than me because she was the one who had been doing it for six series and the true competition on the show is among the dancers, not us.

'*Strictly Come Dancing* was the most amazing human experience you can get. You cannot buy an experience like that and it is one of the most cherished chapters in my life. It's fantastical.'

Richard Dunwoody MBE
Lilia Kopylova

As one of Britain's leading ex-jockeys, Richard is used to galloping to the finish line, but this time he is not putting any bets on himself.

'I think that I should just take it one step at a time and enjoy it and make sure that my dance partner enjoys it too,' he says. 'I have got huge reservations but it's too late now!'

Horses were in Richard's blood, growing up in Ireland with his trainer father, George, while his grandfather, Dick Thrale, was a trainer at Epsom. Richard's first big win was at Cheltenham in 1983 and he acquired many more trophies before picking up the ultimate prize by winning the 1986 Grand National on West Tip.

He went on to team up with national favourite Desert Orchid and together they tasted victory in two King George VI races and the Irish Grand National.

At the forefront of National Hunt racing throughout the 1980s and '90s, Richard was Champion Jockey between 1993 and 1995 and was awarded an MBE in 1993. He retired in 1999 due to an arm injury but retained the record for the most wins in the UK until 2002, when Tony McCoy overtook him.

Although he's looking forward to the show, he feels the spotlight will be much harsher on a *Strictly Come Dancing* contestant than a jockey.

'On this show you have to take critisism on the chin, if you've done all you can. As sportsmen we are quite lucky in horse racing as nine times out of ten we don't get criticised – it is not directed at the jockeys because you can always blame the horse!' he laughs.

As well as the equestrian training, the lean 45 year old has kept himself fit for his many gruelling fund-raising expeditions. Seven years ago he trekked to the Arctic and a year later he entered the Polar Race, a 400-mile journey to the magnetic North Pole, with his team finishing second. Last year, the resilient rider took part in a 48-day trek to the South Pole with American explorer Doug Stoup, raising £100000 for charity. In May 2009, Richard started a 1000 Mile Challenge to walk the same mile 1000 consecutive times for 1000 consecutive hours and again raised over £100000.

Surely all his adventures have prepared him for the difficult task ahead?

'I'm fit to do one or two things,' he says. 'Being fit to dance is something totally different. Whether it's riding a horse or running or pulling a sled, it's such a different type of fitness.

'We have got people like Joe Calzaghe, with his fantastic footwork – he is probably right at the top of the list of the lads.

Richard has been travelling alot so has had little time to worry about what lies ahead, but he isn't too worried.

'I love the show and I hope that I can't be worse in three weeks than I am now. '

'I have done no dancing at all. I will work really hard at it and just get in the studio and do as best as I can. There is a lot to go through.'

Richard's used to wearing the silks, so the Latin shirts shouldn't come as too much of a shock to him, but with absolutely no dancing experience, the choreography might.

'I have had a couple of girlfriends who have been quite good dancers but sadly they have not been able to teach me anything about it,' he says. 'I have not had any training at all in my life. Dancing is not my forte but I wish I had learned to dance!'

As the first jockey to swap the gallops for the foxtrot, Richard has been teamed with series-three winner Lilia Kopylova.

'I am a fan of the show,' he says. 'The great thing about this show is that you are learning a new skill, which really sets it apart from many other shows on TV. Darren Gough, dancing with Lilia, showed the way – so no pressure!'

Lilia Kopylova

Latin champ Lilia has hidden talents – before becoming a professional dancer she was Moscow's figure-skating champ! At 12 she was Russian Ten Dance (combined Latin and ballroom) Champion and in 1997, after moving to London, she began to dance with Darren Bennett, now her husband and fellow *Strictly* professional.

Lilia joined the show in series two and has had many highs and lows since then, from crashing out with the less-than-elegant Dominic Littlewood to winning the trophy with dark horse Darren Gough.

What is it like working with your husband?

We have two separate lives – professional and private. We may fight a bit on the floor during the practice, but when we leave the dance hall everything is behind us, it's gone, it's forgotten. With your professional and private lives, one is one and the other is the other.

How did it feel to win SCD?

To start with I didn't think Darren would get very far. It never once entered my head we would win.

Working with Darren was perfect – he's so easy to teach and we had really fun sessions but worked incredibly hard. Darren was great to work with as he is a sportsperson so knew how to handle competition and recognise the importance of working together as a team.

What was series six like for you?

Don Warrington was a wonderful and very hard-working man – unfortunately it all got too nerve-wracking for him on show days, which made him forget his steps. He was physically shaking – what a shame.

Did you enjoy the tour?

I danced with Julian Clary, which was truly amazing! We had a ball dancing together and Julian was the most energising celebrity partner I've ever had.

I find it very funny and amusing that one of the main characters in Julian Clary's new book is named after me! Julian was writing the book during the *Strictly Come Dancing* tour and named his eccentric ex-cabaret singer character Lilia!

Strictly
Made to Measure

For a *Strictly* contestant, the costume is as much a part of the show as the dance. The right dress, the sexy heels and the fabulous hairstyle can give a performer a huge dose of confidence on the night and even the guys admit that a Latin shirt and Cuban heels can get them in the mood!

But behind each fabulous outfit is a huge amount of skill, patience and man (and woman) hours, and the process starts way before the first dance steps have been taken. So here is your step-by-step guide to the making of a *Strictly Come Dancing* dress.

THE STORY OF LISA'S TANGO DRESS

STEP 1

In July, as soon as the celebrity dancer is confirmed, and even before she has met her dance partner, she sits down with stylist Su Judd and the team of five designers and works out all the dresses for the whole series.

The team will take her measurements and discuss the styles she prefers to wear herself, what she believes looks good on her and any areas that she might feel she wants to cover up. Jo Irvine was the designer who came up with the concept for Lisa's week-seven tango dress.

STEP 2

After two or three hours with Lisa, covering ideas for all 15 dresses she will wear throughout the series, Jo discusses colours with Su Judd and comes up with an initial sketch for the dress.

'The design of the tango dress has to be a weighty skirt because the movement is very staccato,' says Su. 'The catwalk at the time was very much about clashing colours so the jade and tangerine were very obvious when I was looking at the fabrics together. Such vibrant colours are very unusual for the tango.'

STEP 3

Each dress is built around a basic leotard such as a gymnast would wear. The bra cups are then added and the fabric sewn on top.

'The basic make-up really is sportswear,' says Su. 'And on top of that we create an amazing gown.'

STEP 4

Two weeks before the night of the performance, Lisa goes for her first fitting.

meeting with designers
July 2008

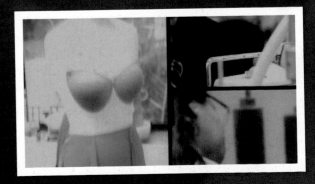

'Even though it's still in the very beginning stages, you can see how it's going to come together,' says Lisa. 'The process is so exciting.'

'Lisa was so delicious to dress because she's lean and long,' Su reveals. 'As soon as that limp piece of Lycra gets on her, it takes shape and becomes something amazing.'

STEP 5

At the first fitting, seams are taken in and the designer alters the shape and cut of the dress. 'Over the series dancers do tend to lose weight, doing all the exercise and training,' reveals Jo. 'Lisa lost weight over her hips, so we had to take that area in.'

'At the fitting, the reason it is couture becomes clear,' explains Su. 'We actually make the dress on her!'

Jo decided at this point that Lisa's long back could be accentuated more so she cut away a section about the bottom to make it more 'sexy and open'.

'The boob area is really important,' reveals Lisa. 'Basically we didn't wear bras but there is a cup area and it's all put in with a strap underneath that lifts up the boobs.'

After the initial fitting, that's when the real craftsmanship begins to happen,' says Su. 'Lisa's tango dress for example had 7700 stones on it – that can take up to 15 hours with two people working very hard.'

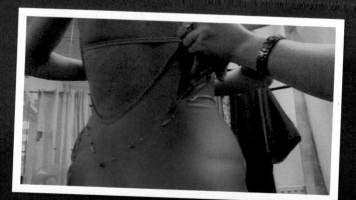

STEP 6

Dance day, and Lisa gets to see the outfit in its full glory for the very first time. With five hours to go until the broadcast, a team of seamstresses and dressers are still sewing in microphone packs and making last-minute adjustments to the dress.

'It still needs a bit of tweaking because it doesn't fit exactly everywhere,' says a worried Lisa. 'We're still kind of making it. I'd be lying if I said I wasn't slightly panicked because I want it to fit like a glove.'

'I am panicking. She's being very positive!' laughs Su. 'Sometimes it really can be up to the last minute.'

STEP 7

Two hours before the show the beautiful jade and tangerine dress gets a final tweaking from dresser Monica Elbs. Brendan Cole, who like many professionals has strong ideas about what his partner should wear, has not yet seen the dress.

'There really isn't enough time to show the boys what their girl is going to wear and they don't like that,' Su reveals. 'But that's just the way it is.'

STEP 8

The dress is finally finished and an anxious Brendan gets to see 'the reveal'. Lisa waits nervously for the verdict.

'I think I like it,' he tells his relieved partner. 'I was fretting because I was told the dress was green and I thought, Green and orange – tango, no. Tango is black, red, deep colours. But that's a stunning dress. You look amazing.' Phew!

STEP 9

The final step is on to the dance floor for a triumphant tango, which Len declared 'superb', Craig 'fantastic' and Bruno 'simply irresistible!'

'I loved every second of the dance and it's all down to the dress,' gushes an ecstatic Lisa. 'It fits like a glove. Yes!'

'On Saturday, when I watch the show, I'm so proud of the team that I work with and feel absolutely elated,' says Su, smiling.

After the dance is over, and the dress cleaned, most of them go back to the headquarters of Dance Sport International in Croydon where the BBC design team work where they can be sold.

Last year, Rachel's salsa dress was exported to Jordan and TV presenter Christine Bleakley's gold tango dress sold for £1900.

Lisa's tango dress, however, was bought by *Best Magazine* and was given away to a fortunate competition winner.

Let's hope it's had a few outings on the dance floor since then.

SUITS YOU, SIR!

It's not just the girls who get to glam it up for the dance. The men might not have such a stunning array of costumes but the cut of the cloth is just as important to their performance.

'It's only when the guys are comfortable with their costume that they can feel comfortable with the dance,' explains stylist Su.

'Boys have a ballroom suit that is made just for them, which will last them for the whole series. They

tend to wear it whatever they are doing. Tony Brackley is the ballroom suit maker; he makes the tail suits. He's ex-Savile Row so he is an absolutely brilliant tailor.'

Tony meets the celebrities as soon as possible to take a series of measurements and then makes a paper pattern. He then cuts the cloth and pins it together for a first fitting.

As the tail-suit jacket is cut high, the trousers have to be very high-waisted to avoid gapping in between the jacket and trouser, which means an 18-inch fly! Simon Cowell eat your heart out.

'Oh my God, the fly on the tail-suit trousers – I've never seen anything like it!' laughs Tom Chambers. 'But the thing that matters the most is the jacket. It just moulds you into the right shape. Normally when you raise your arms you get a bump on the shoulder but here they are so clever that it's a bit tight when you have your arms down but when your raise your arms it stays flat, so you keep the line. It's all about the line.

Latin Lotharios

'When it comes to being daring in *Strictly*, it's all about the Latin,' says Su Judd, and those guys love nothing more than a slinky satin number or a glittering singlet.

'The flamboyancy of costumes, if anything, just helped me,' recalls Tom. 'You feel almost like you're in fancy dress so you can get away with it.'

The design of the shirt is led by the colour of the lady's dress and is put together by Thomas Pearson, an ex-professional Latin dancer who has now turned his talents to dancewear. 'I normally make 20 to 30 costumes per series and the Latin trousers and shirts,' he says. 'I make them all from scratch, and a shirt will take roughly four to five hours from beginning to end.'

Ever wondered how the shirt stays tightly tucked in with all that wiggling and shimmying? Here's a trade secret from Thomas: 'We take a pair of cycling shorts and attach them to the bottom of the shirt to stop the shirt

Shoe Must Be Joking

The biggest shock for the boys is often the size of the Cuban heels they have to wear in the Latin. Unless they've had a starring role in *La Cage aux Folles*, chances are they've never worn heels like this before – especially not to dance in.

'When the male celebrities start in *SCD* I don't think they understand exactly what they're in for,' explains Su. 'Their shoes are their first step into their *Strictly* transformation. The Latin shoes have a one and a half inch heel and the ballroom are a shiny pair of shoes with an inch heel.'

from coming out of the trousers when you are dancing.'

Many of the Latin shirts are covered in glittering crystals of varying colours, which are painstakingly glued on by hand. On average it takes three hours to stone a shirt and approximately 8000 stones are used per shirt.

Stoner Elise Rumary explains: 'It's rare that we use sequins. They are tiny glass stones that are glued on one by one. They can be washed but they cannot be put in a tumble dryer because the heat will melt all the stones off.'

'In the Latin shoes you do wobble a bit more, so you kind of feel what it's like to be a lady wearing high-heeled shoes,' recalls Tom. But Austin took it all in his tottering stride: 'They're really comfy actually. Strangely, I've never had any problems with my feet in them.'

After the celebrities are issued with their shoes, they are theirs for the series and it is their responsibility to bring them to every rehearsal and performance.

On dance day, the wardrobe team spend the afternoon ironing, steaming and sewing while the couples rehearse and have make-up applied, eyebrows plucked and hair put into wild Latin or sleeked-back ballroom styles.

'If I had to choose any performance where the hair, make-up and costume made a big difference – it would be all of them,' says Austin Healey.

Su is justifiably proud of her achievements with the male celebs.

'We take these rough diamonds and we turn them into polished performers,' she says. 'When the male celebrities finally become comfortable in the dancing and the costumes together, that's when it all comes good for me. They become peacocks – for me they go over to the "dance side".'

Ricky Groves
Erin Boag

Ricky has had a busy year on Albert Square, with his character Garry Hobbs getting engaged to local beauty Dawn and then dumping her at the altar after finding out about her affair with Phil.

But between filming his emotional scenes in *EastEnders*, Ricky has been keeping a close eye on *Strictly* and has become something of an expert.

'Mark Foster is my neighbour and so I supported him last year. He looked fantastic in some of those costumes but that's because he's trained every day of his life and never eats pizza – the man has suffered for his sport!' he joked. 'I would have loved for him to go further in the competition but he was *Strictly*'s very own Peter Crouch: a bit lanky and graceless but with a boundless amount of energy.

'I believe Tom Chambers deserved to win last year. He showed himself to be a wonderful all-rounder throughout the series.

'It was interesting to note that everybody treated the earlier stages in a very light-hearted way but as soon as the quarter-finals arrived then the remaining dancers became very, very serious.'

Ricky came to his career in acting relatively late, having been a keen amateur all his life.

A Londoner, born in 1968, he first trained as a chef but at the age of 29 decided on a change and enlisted in The Poor School, graduating in 1999 and joining the cast of *EastEnders* as Lynne Slater's beleaguered boyfriend a year later.

After an unsuccessful marriage, Garry went on to have various flings in the Square, one of which was with Laura Beale, played by Hannah Waterman. Off screen the pair fell in love and were married in 2006, making Ricky the son-in-law of actors Dennis Waterman and Patricia Maynard.

Having survived nine years on the BBC soap, which he has now left, he is thrilled to be glamming up on Saturday nights for a change.

'I really do feel like I'm the cat that got the cream at the moment,' he says, beaming. '*Strictly Come Dancing* is an absolutely fantastic show and I'm so proud to be taking part this year. It's a fantastic piece of family entertainment, glamorous and graceful, perfect Saturday-night fodder. I just hope I don't let the series down!'

Like most of the men, he admits to a bit of a boogie when alcohol has been supped, but he has also had a smidgeon of training in the past.

'I attended drama school and experienced a few hours of dance lessons whilst there,' he admits. 'Nothing fancy, though – we were just taught the basics. I remember really enjoying the salsa classes. I loved the rhythm involved.'

And he has danced in front of an audience – albeit not quite 12 million strong!

'A few years ago I acted in a play called *Country Dancing*, which was written by a playwright called Nigel Williams. I had to dance to three different pieces of country music during the show and I loved that experience.

'The run only lasted for ten shows and it wasn't a West End production, but I still got into the role as much as I could.'

Ricky should have some interesting moves on the dance floor, given that he is more influenced by John Travolta than Fred Astaire.

'I was 11 or 12 and *Saturday Night Fever* had just been released,' recalls the 41-year-old actor, who will be dancing with Erin Boag. 'There was an adult-certificate movie but they also released a more family-friendly version. I watched that with some friends and absolutely loved John Travolta and the moves he pulled. I would love to dance to some of those tunes on *Strictly*!'

Ricky is keen to learn as many dances as he can and is also itching to get at the spangled shirts.

'I'm looking forward to every single dance on the show but I have to admit to being very excited about attempting the jive,' he says. 'Jill Halfpenny's jive was absolutely fantastic and has cast a long shadow but I'm looking to have some fun with that one.

'I'm also looking forward to experimenting with all sorts of costumes as the weeks go on,' he confesses. 'I will possibly indulge myself with a tan or two but do warn me if I start turning into David Dickinson!'

Erin Boag

Although she has yet to pick up the trophy, Erin has twice made it to the final of *Strictly Come Dancing*, in series two with comedian Julian Clary and again the following year with Colin Jackson.

In series six, she and rugby player Austin Healey were knocked out in the quarter-finals.

As the daughter of a professional dance couple, the sparky New Zealander was destined to follow in their elegant footsteps and decided she wanted to put her all into it when she saw a dance competition at the age of 15. She began dancing with Anton Du Beke in 1997.

Was series six a good experience?

I have never laughed so much in my life. We had the best time but both of us were so upset when we got knocked out so close to the end. We worked so hard I can't begin to tell you what it feels like when they tell you you're out of the competition. I cried for the first time in six series.

Have you danced with Austin since?

When Anton had to have an emergency operation earlier this year, we had corporate shows booked, which we could not cancel. I had to call on Austin to save the day. I never thought I would be standing on the dance floor ready to perform corporate shows with one of my celebrity partners. Austin was great and brought the house down. In one show I called him Anton by mistake. He now has the nickname Austin Du Beke.

When did you start dancing?

I guess like many little girls, I wanted to dance! Mum took me as a three year old to dance classes, where I began learning ballet, tap, jazz, ballroom and Latin. Through my teens, I was also a really keen sportsgirl and loved many different sports – I represented my school in swimming, hockey, netball, football, trampoline and athletics!

Favourite dance?

I love the quickstep. It's fast, it's bright and definitely my favourite – it also brings back memories of being in the final with Julian and Colin. In Latin, I like the cha cha cha because it's sexy but also very cheeky.

Who would be your ideal celeb?

I can work with most people – if they are willing to learn and have good concentration then I am happy. As always I would like to have a great time with someone who will give me 100 per cent commitment. I have been lucky and danced with some wonderful men. Of course I would be lying if I didn't say I am hoping for Brad Pitt!

Best moment of the last year?

I am very lucky and married the most wonderful man in the world in June this year in Italy. It was the best day of my life.

THE MARCH OF THE SERGEANT

Everybody loves an underdog and the annals of *Strictly* history are littered with celebs with two left feet who have clung on to their dancing shoes in spite of consistently low scores. Chris Parker paso dobled his way into the heart of the nation and into the final in series one; Kate Garraway went through the mill, with injuries and low scores, stumbling her way into week seven, and Julian Clary joked his way into the series-two final.

But one man caused more of a furore than any other before him, as the dances became increasingly hilarious and the public voted him back on the show time and time again – John Sergeant.

Arlene told him, 'You are outstanding at dancing really badly,' and Craig branded him a 'disaster!' But still he continued to avoid the dance-off.

Even before he set foot on the dance floor, John was enchanting the nation with his schoolboy giggles and witty one-liners. On meeting his dance partner, the beautiful Kristina Rihanoff, he joked, 'For a serious political journalist like me to suddenly hitch up with this fantastic girl … Gosh. I do like being a dancer, you know.' And he took advantage of the fact that the sultry Siberian was new to the country as he sniggered, 'Kristina doesn't know much about me so I have overegged the CV a bit.'

The Judges on John

On the week-three tango:
Len: 'Craig said your posture's poor. Once you get to a certain age your posture is always going to be poor. She's only a dance teacher, not a miracle worker.'

On the week six paso doble:
Bruno: 'Dad's Army does the paso!'
Len: 'Sergeant, after all that marching you should be demoted to a private!'
Craig: 'You took marching to a whole new level.'

On the week-seven foxtrot:
Len: 'I can't have a go at some of the others about poor technique and then forget about it with you. It's not Help The Aged!'

In turn, Kristina told the viewers, 'I guess I didn't know how big John is in this country. He's a very famous and respected man!'

John's first dance was a promising waltz, which the judges were enthralled by.

'It was so cute and cuddly it was like watching Winnie the Pooh and Tigger,' commented Bruno. 'It was so endearing.' Even Craig called it 'a very warm and honest performance' while Len observed, 'Sometimes a whisper conveys more than a shout. It was quiet and it was charming.'

Little did anyone know that this whisper was merely the calm before the storm!

Things started to go downhill with the week-three tango, which Bruno compared to 'a father after a couple of pints' and Arlene commented, 'You came in with all the drama of Peter Mandelson's return to the cabinet and then started to enjoy yourself too much.'

Still, a score of 22 kept him off the bottom spot and the public once more kept him out of the dance-off. With Phil Daniels and Gary Rhodes gone, however, things began to look grim in week five when his samba left him at the bottom of the leader board.

Again, phone votes allowed him to return the following week with his *pièce de résistance*, the paso doble, which saw him dragging the long-suffering Kristina around like a sack of spuds.

The judges hated it; the nation loved it. It even got a mention on *Newsnight*, with the comment, 'John Sergeant single-handedly lifts the mood of the nation.' However, the judges were getting frustrated. John's week-eight cha cha cha was, according to Bruce, 'being anticipated in different ways by different people. Ten million viewers up and down the country can't wait to see it and four judges wish they didn't have to!'

The routine started with John miming a telephone call, which in turn sent Len into something of a rant. 'I'll tell you what the phone call was about. He was phoning his mates to tell them to vote for him because if they don't he's got no chance!

'John, I like you but if someone really deserving gets knocked out, it makes a nonsense of the show. I don't like to say it but it's true.'

Even Kristina was making wisecracks about his lack of ability. When Bruce asked how John could look at her and remember the steps at the same time, Kristina quipped, 'He doesn't!'

After a paltry one from Craig (who snapped, 'If I had a zero it would have come out') the couple landed the lowest score of the series with 12, but the fight hadn't gone out of John just yet.

'The problem with us going any further is the effect it will have on the judges,' he joked. 'Some of them are elderly and they may not be able to cope.'

After week nine's American smooth, which received some positive comments and gained a score of 22, John dropped the bombshell. On 19 November he called a press conference and quit the show citing 'a real danger that I might win the competition. Even for me that would be a joke too far.

'We had fun dancing and dancing is a wonderfully enjoyable thing, but if the joke wears thin, if people begin to take things very seriously, then it is time to go.' On week ten John returned to waltz off into the sunset with a final dance – and no judges' comments to spoil the moment.

Martina Hingis
Matthew Cutler

In theory, tennis players should fare well in the *Strictly* challenge given their athleticism, lightning reactions and fast footwork on the court – but tell that to Andrew Castle …

Martina Hingis is notorious for her finesse and style so she should get the ball back in her court in no time at all. The Wimbledon singles winner has also notched up three Australian wins and one US Open victory as well as nine Grand Slam women's doubles titles. Yet she is hoping to emulate another impressive lady – our very own Alesha Dixon. Luckily she is dancing with Alesha's winning partner Matthew Cutler.

'I have seen some of the Alesha Dixon dances on the internet,' says the Swiss sensation. 'She was a very, very graceful dancer. Let us hope that one day I may dance like her!'

The discipline of training will come as second nature to the 28 year old. The daughter of two professional tennis players, she was named after Martina Navratilova and started playing when she was just two years old. She was competing at four and, at 12, became the youngest player to win a Grand Slam junior title when she scooped the girls' singles at the French Open. A year later she won the girls' singles title at Wimbledon, and reached the final of the US Open.

After turning professional at 14, she won a total of 43 Women's Tennis Association Tour singles titles and 37 Women's Tennis Association doubles titles before announcing a break from the game in 2002 due to a recurring ligament injury in both ankles. In January 2006 she returned to the court, only to retire again in November of the following year due to health problems.

Now Martina is keen to try out her fleet of foot on the floor; although she is no longer on the tennis circuit, she is still competing with some of her well-known opponents.

'I love watching dancing. It is a very hard skill to learn,' she concedes. 'Some of the other players on the tennis circuit have done other versions in different countries. Monica Seles competed in the US version and had a blast. She didn't make it very far in the competition though. I hope to get further than she did!

'The internet has been very useful to me as I've looked at all the different dances performed on lots of international versions of the show and that's given me plenty to think about. It has helped with my education of what is in store for me!

'I should be good with the training as I am used to working very hard for many hours to perfect my

sport. Discipline is very important when training for tennis competitions and I think this will be the same when preparing for the Saturday dance.'

Although as a child Martina started some lessons in her home town of Zurich, she soon became focused on tennis.

'I come from the suburbs of Zurich where there are only a few opportunities to dance,' she says. 'There was no special school and many of my friends did not dance. I took ballet when I was very young – however, I am unable to remember at what age or anything from that time. I had to stop the classes as tennis became my life.

'All my time had to be spent on the tennis courts rather than on the dance floors. Now I am doing this show I wish I had experienced many more dance lessons!'

And she is keen to swap the whites for something more eye-catching.

'I am really excited by the prospect of wearing many colourful and pretty costumes. I really cannot wait to begin!'

The 'Swiss miss' is confident she can handle the judges and says their criticism couldn't be worse than her mum's.

'I was a professional sportswoman for many years and played against the very top names in the world,' she says. 'Criticism was always hard to take in tennis because I knew I had the skill and should always win. Now that I am doing your show I know I will not be the best in the field and so will prepare myself for criticism. That will be fair if I have been bad.

'It is normal for me to be the best I can and I will try to excel but when it comes to criticism I think the judges will be nothing compared to how my mum used to be during tennis! I hope that is not the case anyway.'

Matthew Cutler

Latin champ Matthew started competing at the age of ten and by 14 he was ranked number-one junior in the UK and undefeated champion in all the major competitions.

After meeting ex-partner Nicole in his late teens, the couple were soon in the world top six and went on to become World, European and International Champions as well as taking the British title five times.

Matthew's debut on *Strictly*, in series three, was something of a disappointment as he and actress Siobhan Hayes were voted out after their first dance.

He more than made up for it in series five, twirling his way to a stunning final and sharing the trophy with Alesha Dixon. Last year he got to week 11 with *The One Show* presenter Christine Bleakley.

How did it feel to win *SCD*?

Winning *Strictly Come Dancing* was like a dream come true for me. Alesha was amazing – she had the rare balance of dedication, fun and talent. The whole experience was mad, exciting, exhausting – I loved it!

How was series six for you?

There was never a dull moment with Christine Bleakley. I didn't think it was possible to laugh the same as I did with Alesha, but I did with Christine. Our personalities are practically the same so we clicked instantly. We worked hard but also kept it fun. Perfect!

Favourite dance?

I feel I can really get into the jive as it's a relaxed dance and not very controlled and restricted. It's also the dance I was known for in the competitive circuit. In ballroom it has to be the quickstep. It's just such a fast-paced, lively and happy dance, definitely my favourite ballroom.

How did you first get into dancing?

I was always interested in dancing and jumping around to music. I used to ride to dance classes, which were held in the local church every Saturday. I used to come home from dancing and show my mum what I had learned (she had a basic knowledge of Latin and ballroom dances). I used to practise at home and by the next week I would show the teachers my routine and they couldn't believe how good I was – it was all due to Mum really but they thought I just had a natural talent for it, which I suppose I did.

Career highlight?

Winning the World Amateur Championships with Nicole in 1999. It is every dancer's dream to become a world champion and you work so hard to achieve it, practising as much as possible, having private coaching.

So when you do eventually win the title it is a mixture of complete relief that the competition is over and sheer joy and amazement that you now hold the title and it can never be taken away from you. It is also a great help to have the title or to have been a world champion as a lot of work comes from it.

Ideal celeb?

I need a partner who believes in what I say and is prepared to try anything. I would also like her to have an opinion about what she wants to look like and perform like on the dance floor, which would help me to create the perfect choreography.

My worst fear would be someone who just couldn't be bothered!

Strictly Crossword

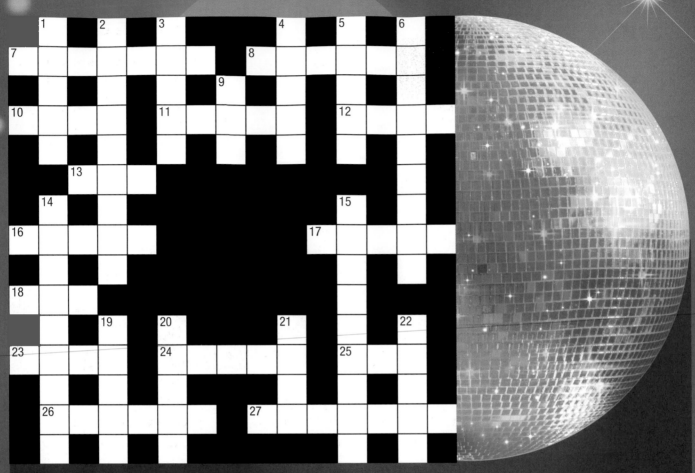

Across

7 See 20D

8 Actress known for *EastEnders* and *The Bill* who came fourth in series four with Vincent (6)

10 Former England cricketer who followed in 4D's footsteps by scooping the *Strictly* title (4)

11 Waspish *Strictly* judge known for saying 'It was a disaaahster!' (5)

12 Name shared by *Strictly* runners-up Mr Dawson and Mr DiAngelo (4)

13 *Strictly*'s head judge, who's also on the US version with 20A (3)

16 *Casualty* actress who teamed up with Brendan Cole for series two (5)

17 *Strictly* pro who went from victory with 10A to crashing out in week one with Brian Capron (5)

18 Andrew Castle's dance partner, whose husband is *Strictly* pro James (3)

23 Former Liverpool footballer who partnered Nicole Cutler in series five (4)

24 & 3D British athlete turned pundit who made it to week six with Camilla Dallerup in series two (5,5)

25 Onetime *Corrie* star who reached the same point with the same partner as 24A (3)

26 Former snooker ace who was a hit with fans if not judges alongside 21D in series five (6)

27 *Bad Girls* star who competed alongside 15D and winner Robbie Earle in *Strictly African Dancing* (7)

Down

1 Sports presenter who shocked fans when she was knocked out of *Strictly* before husband Kenny (5)

2 Presenter who hosts *Strictly Come Dancing: It Takes Two* (9)

3 See 24A

4 Former England cricketer who won series three of *Strictly* (5)

5 Veteran comedian who pulled out of series four due to ill-health (5)

6 Dancer who partnered Christopher Parker to second place in series one (9)

9 Lofty dance pro who reached *Strictly* finals with Denise Lewis and Zoe Ball (3)

14 Actress known as Walford's Kathy, who followed fellow *EastEnder* Phil Daniels out of series six (9)

15 Former athlete who took part in the 2005 spin-off *Strictly African Dancing* (9)

19 *Strictly* pro who has become a presenter in his own right (5)

20 & 7A Exuberant *Strictly* judge who has choreographed for Sting, Elton John, The Rolling Stones and Bananarama (5,7)

21 Dance pro who got a third place with Julian Clary and was runner-up with Colin Jackson (4)

22 Name shared by series-one dance pro Miss Jones and Miss Minogue, who sang on *Strictly* in 2007 (5)

Strictly Wordsearch

Strictly Spot the Difference

Look at these two pictures closely and see if you can find ten differences between them.

AMERICAN SMOOTH
BALLROOM
CHA-CHA-CHA
CHOREOGRAPHY
COSTUME
DANCE OFF
FOXTROT
JIVE
LATIN
MAMBO
PASO DOBLE
QUICKSTEP
ROUTINE
RUMBA
SALSA
SAMBA
STEPS
SWING
TANGO
VIENNESE WALTZ

C	H	O	R	E	O	G	R	A	P	H	Y	S	Y	S
O	E	E	O	G	N	I	W	S	T	T	X	T	I	B
M	O	O	R	L	L	A	B	S	O	O	H	E	L	E
P	R	O	U	T	I	N	E	O	K	O	A	P	I	E
Q	A	J	N	A	C	F	E	J	C	M	I	S	A	S
U	E	S	I	S	S	V	F	T	T	S	S	S	C	E
I	O	E	O	V	A	A	E	O	M	N	L	H	N	U
C	E	M	N	D	E	M	R	C	E	A	A	A	I	E
K	S	U	O	L	O	T	B	E	S	C	E	K	T	S
S	R	T	K	B	X	B	T	A	H	I	N	E	A	R
T	I	S	H	O	M	A	L	A	R	R	D	A	L	A
E	R	O	F	P	N	A	C	E	O	E	S	E	D	E
P	I	C	O	G	I	H	M	R	U	M	B	A	I	O
T	L	Z	O	O	A	E	T	O	A	A	A	O	E	L
T	V	I	E	N	N	E	S	E	W	A	L	T	Z	L

Chris Hollins
Ola Jordan

As well as the chance to dance, Chris has an unusual motive behind his decision to take part in *Strictly Come Dancing*.

'I'm looking forward to meeting my all-time hero: Mr Bruce Forsyth!' reveals the BBC sports presenter. 'I've been an enormous fan of his since I was a little boy. *The Generation Game* was my favourite show ever and I can't believe I'll soon be on stage with him!'

And winning the glitter-ball trophy isn't the only dream he would like to see come true.

'I have seen Bruce on the odd golf course. I'm a keen golfer myself. But our paths have only crossed in the bar afterwards. I've never played him. Playing golf with Bruce Forsyth? That would be my ultimate dream!'

Born in Bromley, Kent, Chris grew up around sport. His father, John, played for Chelsea, Arsenal and England and Uncle David was a goalie for Newcastle United and Wales. After leaving school, Chris played for Charlton, Queens Park Rangers and Aldershot Town before going back to university, in Durham and then Oxford, where he played first-class cricket. In 1994, Chris kick-started his broadcasting career with a job on Sky Sports.

After spells with GMTV, Meridian and Five.tv, the respected journalist moved to the BBC in 1999 and joined the *BBC Breakfast* team in 2005.

Chris, who is dancing with the stunning Ola Jordan, says his excitement at being in the show is tinged with apprehension.

'When the phone rings and you are told you are in *Strictly Come Dancing* you are so excited to be part of such a big event,' he recalls. 'You put the phone down and about ten seconds later you realise what you've let yourself in for – hard training, dancing in front of millions of people and the fear of falling flat on your face.'

But he was never in any doubt that he wanted to try his moves on the dance floor.

'I'm a huge, huge fan of the show. Every year the show gets better and better and I'm hoping to continue that tradition this year,' he says.

'I've always wanted to learn how to dance and this is the perfect opportunity. I'll be a pupil with the best teachers in their field and am incredibly keen to start my training as soon as possible.'

Strictly won't be the first time he's strutted his stuff in front of the TV cameras.

'I've done the odd dance for Children In Need. A couple of years ago Carol Kirkwood [BBC weathergirl] and I had to ice skate to the Scissor Sisters' "I Don't Feel Like Dancin'" at Somerset House. We had very little rehearsal, the temperature was freezing and we were terrible.

'Then, last year, I took part in the traditional BBC newsreaders Children In Need dance in the studio. We performed a routine to "Dancing Queen" live on the night in front of a studio audience. I was wearing the full West End gear. Tight spandex trousers, colour top, high collars. Not a pretty sight!'

And he has already had a taste of what's in store from the judges.

'I work with professional sportsmen and so fully appreciate that the best way to deal with criticism is to take it on the chin – or in my case, two chins!

'As long as what they say is fair then I'll take it. They're normally very good at being constructive; they explain why they thought something was bad and that's something I can learn from.

'I can understand why some people do get angry with them. Imagine the scenario: you've just danced for a couple of minutes in front of several million people and so you're bound to feel emotional and in a tender state.

'When I did the Children In Need ice-skate dance, *BBC Breakfast* had some of the *Strictly* judges as guests in the studio. My producer decided it would be fun for them to see my performance on the ice. Whilst Len and Bruno were fairly generous, Craig was brutal. So I've already experienced the sharp tongue of the judges!'

Chris follows a long line of breakfast-TV presenters who, with the exception of series-one winner Natasha Kaplinsky, have not fared too well. But Chris reckons he'll be happy if he just gets further than his colleague Bill Turnbull.

And, apart from falling flat on his face, the 38 year old has one other fear.

'The one thing I'm really scared of – and I'm not going to do – is fake tan!'

Ola Jordan

Polish star Ola started dancing at 12 and her teachers immediately spotted her natural talent. Six months later she was competing and winning regional youth contests. At 17, she won the Open Polish Championship, travelled to the World Championships the same year and in April 2000 James Jordan called and asked if she would consider a try-out with him.

The couple matched perfectly and married in 2003. Joining *SCD* for series four, Ola was disappointed when she and DJ Spoony were third to be eliminated. She had better luck with Scottish rugby star Kenny Logan, who tackled his way through to show nine in series five, and suffered from the GMTV curse when it came to Andrew Castle, who survived until show seven.

Describe your three celebrity partners

Spoony was amazing. He was such a fun guy and made me laugh all the time. He knew how much work was needed to stay in the competition.

Kenny wasn't the best dancer but he was a lovely person; he really made the show for me. I enjoyed every minute. I loved spending time with him.

What can I say about Andrew? Well, he was a better tennis player than he was a dancer but he had a sportsman's mentality, which meant he never gave up.

Is there rivalry between you and James?

There is a bit of competition between us, of course, but we both want each other to do the best we can. But I do want to win!

Last year James got further in the series than me. This year I want him to see me lifting the trophy. I am looking forward to putting the *Strictly* glitterball on my bedside cabinet so James has to look at it every night before he goes to bed!

What's your teaching style?

Sweet and quiet in the beginning and then I'll be much stronger once I get to know my celebrity. If they need a kick, I would give them that. I'm not afraid to be nasty if that's what it takes.

Ideal celeb?

Someone who I would feel comfortable with. I think Peter Andre would be fabulous. You spend a lot of time with your celebrity, and it is wonderful when you partner someone with a lovely personality. I would also like to have someone who loves dancing just as much as I do.

I am quiet and shy off the dance floor, but once I'm on the floor I relax and become extremely open when I dance. Someone who has real confidence will help us on the dance floor and we'll form a great partnership.

Favourite dance?

The samba is without doubt my favourite dance – it's fast, it's rhythmical and there is so much body movement. I'm fun and bouncy and I think that's exactly what the samba is all about.

A WEEK IN THE

Behind the scenes of a dancing sensation

LIFE OF SCD

To the millions of viewers who settle down on their sofas for their weekly glamour fix, *Strictly Come Dancing* is a weekend treat. But for the celebrities, professionals and the huge production team, the show is an all-consuming passion and a 24/7 occupation.

Even before the first programme is aired in September, their lives are filled with dress fittings, music discussions, logistics and, for the celebs, the dreaded weeks of pre-training. The first training sessions start three weeks before the first broadcast, by which time the celebrities have been kitted out with their shoes and sometimes, for the girls, a rehearsal skirt, and musical director David Arch is already working his way through a long list of tracks.

'We start in August thinking about music,' says senior live producer Liz Trott. 'The dancers suggest tracks that they've heard early on; we listen to all the music with them and pick what we use. There are always certain songs in the charts at the time which everyone suggests so it's first come first served – the first dancer to suggest it, gets it.

'David Arch and his engineer will then start putting together the edited version as early as possible.

'The costume designers start working with the celebrities as soon as they are signed up. Even before that Su and her team are looking at ideas, seeing what's on the catwalk and how that might translate and what styles are in and out in the Latin and ballroom dance world and designing costumes for the group dances.

'The set will also be redesigned with the set designer and any changes to the backstage areas, colours and décor will be discussed.'

And from the moment the famous theme tune announces the start of the new series, the *Strictly* machine moves at full throttle from September to Christmas. Here's a typical week behind the scenes of our favourite Saturday-night show.

SUNDAY

After the excitement of the night before, the exhausted celebs undoubtedly deserve a day of rest. They should be so lucky!

'Most of the couples train from Monday through to Friday,' reveals senior celebrity producer Charlotte Oates. 'But some people train on Sundays and quite often we have rehearsals for the group dances, so it is incredibly full on.

'Some people like to be in the training room as often as they can and others like to limit it. We ask for a minimum of 12 hours a week but as time goes on people tend to do a lot more than 12 hours.

'There's hard work in store for the set builders too. Because the show shares its Television Centre studio with several other BBC programmes, everything from the light riggings to the dance floor has to be taken down and stored away in another part of the complex.

MONDAY AND TUESDAY

For the few lucky souls who managed to relax on Sunday, it's back to work first thing on Monday. As Tom Chambers remembers all too well, this can bring about a Monday-morning feeling familiar to workers everywhere.

'You experience a huge sense of relief, having completed a dance on Saturday night, but you soon realise that you have to start all over again with a new dance on Monday,' he recalls.

'Monday was always a black day because it was like starting at the bottom of the valley and trying to climb up to the top of a mountain all over again. You felt there was no way you were going to be ready by Saturday night.

'The audience tunes in at the weekend and watches another dance but they don't realise what you've been through that week. It's like learning to fly an aeroplane because there are so many new styles and checks you have to make – your elbows, your shoulders, your line, your head, where your bodyweight is going as well as the steps. It's absolutely exhausting.'

While the couples work on their choreography, the production staff are busy working out the logistics for the next show.

'For the early part of the week, I am putting the script together with our script writer,' reveals Liz. 'Because a lot of Bruce's gags are based on what's happened the week before, Bruce comes up with ideas early in the week and I will start putting together the basics of the script.

'Tess and the team also start thinking about the types of questions she might want to ask the celebrities, based on their stories and what's happening in training, injuries and previous scores.

'The order in which people will perform also needs to be worked out. At the start of the series we have the same styles of dance so in week one it might be cha cha cha and waltz. We alternate those dances but we also have to decide who would be a good person to open the show, the best music to open with and who would be good to close the show.

'The order is about the couple, their story, the music and their dance – for example, you might not want to start a show with a slow waltz but something lively like a cha cha cha.

WEDNESDAY

Provided the set was taken down the week before, the reconstruction process begins late on Wednesday with the arrival of the huge light riggings in the 10,500 square foot of studio space known as TC1.

As well as the hundreds of fixed lights overhead, there are banks of 'specials', which follow the dancers around the floor. These have to be programmed and controlled from the director's gallery and must be wired up before the rest of

the set can be built. Electricians and technicians work through the night to complete the job in time for the set build the following day.

THURSDAY

From 6am, the familiar set starts to reappear. The famous double staircase that first reveals the 16 celebrities is built, followed by the curtained area where Tess interviews the couples after their dances. Then the orchestra area, the judges' area and last but by no means least is the centrepiece – the dance floor.

Designed by production designer Patrick Doherty, it is constructed from plywood and parquet flooring on a metal frame, which sits on a layer of foam to give it the necessary bounce. It breaks down into 20 pieces, which have to be re-laid with painstaking perfection to avoid any possibility of a trip. 'There's a great scenery crew who piece the whole set together,' says Liz. 'Everything

has to be put back together, from the judges' desk to the orchestra area, the stairs and the dance floor.

'The lighting is always being tinkered with, right up to the show, although it is always in place in time for the Friday rehearsal.

'We have had surprisingly few technical hitches considering it's a live show on such a huge scale. There was the incident when Karen Hardy and Mark Ramprakash got their microphones tangled but apart from that I think it's only been minor things, which we may notice but the viewers at home would never know. As it's a live show everyone has to be at the top of their game and it has to be a well-oiled machine.'

In another part of the BBC building, Bruce and Tess are going through the full script for the first time and being given their directions for the following show. Throughout the week the celebrities and professionals will also have been to dress fittings and meetings with hair and make-up to discuss that perfect look.

FRIDAY

As Saturday night looms large, the couples finally get a chance to move their routines on to the *Strictly* dance floor. As the band is not in place, they rehearse to the pre-recorded tracks sent in by David Arch.

'Each couple has about half an hour on the floor,' explains Charlotte Oates. 'As soon as the set goes in and it's safe, I schedule the couples to have their time on the floor with our cameras, staggering their times and working around their schedules.

'It's really important for the couples to have this rehearsal because it's the first time they can do their routines on the actual dance floor.'

It's also a great opportunity for the hair and make-up teams to grab their models for fittings and style meetings.

Bruce and Tess are in the studio during the day for a camera rehearsal. They read through the entire script, which is then fed into the autocue, while the floor manager puts tape on the floor to mark their positions.

SATURDAY

Excitement, anticipation and nerves are the order of the day as the evening's show draws closer. Despite the late night that lies ahead, the devoted team are up with the larks to get everything in place.

'Saturday is a full day,' says Charlotte. 'The girls come in from eight or nine in the morning for hair and make-up and the boys slightly later. The atmosphere is very exciting. It's like the team effort of the week is geared towards that Saturday night.'

During the morning the orchestra play through the tracks together for the first time. Then the costume, music and dance finally come together for the dress rehearsals, where the couples dance to the live track.

'Often hearing a band is different from hearing the CD you've been listening to all week. The band may be asked to go a touch slower or faster. We iron all those things out on Saturday.'

Make-up is retouched all day and adjustments are still being made to dresses and suits right up to the last minute.

The audience begins to arrive outside the building as early as 10am, anxious to get the best seat in the house.

As the dress rehearsals are in full swing, mid afternoon, they are let into the foyer and they come into the studio to be seated just before 5pm.

'When the audience is all in we may use the time to pre-record an item, if for technical reasons it can't be shown live,' says Liz. 'It may be that a guest star is doing a concert that night so we have to record it earlier, or young children are dancing, which means we can't have them performing too late. Sometimes we record things before we go on air, which are then played into the results show. Obviously, we would never pre-record a dance!'

After that the audience is treated to a routine from the hilarious warm-up man, Stuart Holdham, who's a huge *Strictly* fan himself and is a valued part of the team. Shortly before broadcast time, there's another treat as Bruce comes on for his own warm-up.

'Bruce absolutely makes a point of putting some time aside in his schedule so he can meet the audience. In fact he stays on the floor until about a minute before the show starts. That can be quite scary sometimes – once he's on and making the audience laugh he doesn't like to leave so he cuts it a bit fine!'

By this time, the celebrities are backstage, either practising a dodgy step in the corridors or biting their nails in fear!

'The first week they are much more nervous because they've never done it but as the weeks go on they are just incredibly keen to get on the floor. Nobody has yet refused to go out on the night. It's a warm atmosphere as everyone is in the same boat and they all support each other. They also know that their partner is very supportive and they are in safe hands.

'So far, we haven't had anyone who hasn't enjoyed themselves so it's a very positive show.'

With the set in place, the judges seated, the celebs ready to descend the stairs and, hopefully, Tess in her position beside Bruce, there's only one thing left to do – enjoy the show!

Jade Johnson
Ian Waite

Tall, elegant, fit and ultra-competitive, Jade has everything it takes to be a *Strictly* champ. And the lean long-jumper won't have a problem with the outrageous outfits either – she is already famous for the coloured fishnets she wears while competing.

'It started as a bet but has now become a superstition because every time I've not worn them I've jumped poorly,' she reveals.

'The only problem is I like to match. I'd like to wear pink or yellow fishnets but unless my kit matches then I'll have to go for laid-back colours. It is no longer a superstition; it is just part of me.'

The 29-year-old athlete had a tough upbringing in Liverpool and admits that as a 'streetwise, very mouthy and quite boisterous' teenager, she may have gone off the rails without the sports training. The hard work paid off when she bagged the Amateur Athletic Association under-15 title in 1994 and went on to make her international debut in the long jump in 1995.

Now a Commonwealth Games and European Championships silver medallist, she has represented Britain in the last two Olympics. Bizarrely, considering her chosen event, she suffers from an allergy to sand.

'I break out in rashes all over the backs and sides of my legs – massive red blotchy stuff. I've noticed over the years that the gravity of it varies depending on the type of sand.'

Jade, who is paired with Ian Waite, is hoping to gain an advantage through her Olympian fitness training and is currently preparing for 2012 – when she's not in the dance studio.

'I'm doing this because I'm crazy! I think it is so funny!' she laughs. 'As I said to my coach, I've got a couple of years until the Olympics in London in 2012, so I thought I wouldn't properly concentrate on training until January next year. That left me a gap at the end of this year – so I agreed to do *Strictly*.

'I love a challenge and having danced for Sport Relief, with former contestant Roger Black, I know how hard it is.

'My friend is the athlete Maurice Greene, who took part in *Dancing with the Stars* in America last year, so I'm going to call him for advice on

Ian Waite

This year the Reading-bo
Strictly without professic
Dallerup, after she left tl
winning the last series.

Ian started dancing at ten, after his
along to his own Saturday-morning
the girls in the class, fed up with hi
act, dragged him on to the dance
began to compete and, after movi
for four years, he became Dutch P
Champion in 2000.

The tallest of the *Strictly* danc
partnered with the tall, willowy
that has often (though not alwa
advantage. He came second in s
athlete Denise Lewis and third i
with Zoe Ball. Since then he has
Mica Paris, who went out in we
Lancaster Stewart, who fell victi
in week six. In series six, Ian and
it to week ten.

Favourite dance?
The jive, because it is energetic a
ballroom, I like the foxtrot for th
because the music is slow and yc

Ideal celeb?
If I could have all of my previous
one person that would be my id
I'd like someone who wants to l
fun along the way!

how to cope with all the da

Admitting she enjoys 'sh
club', her past dancing expe
different to the foxtrot anc
learning for the show.

'I once appeared as the
on *A Question of Sport* anc
perform as Beyoncé to the
in Love",' she explains. 'It w
an absolute nightmare. I tc
myself after that experienc
that I would never do anyt
that involved choreograph
music in the future – I mus
be mad.

'I went to a club in LA
a week ago and it is half
run by one of the top
choreography dancers in
LA. As a result the club wa
full of great dancers and I
got down with them – I'm
good freestyle dancer to
and R&B, but I suppose th

Craig Kelly
Flavia Cacace

Corrie fans will know Craig as local lothario Luke Strong, but he's hoping he won't be luke-warm on the dance floor.

'I really want to push myself and I want to surprise myself and come away with some good moves,' he says. 'I really hope for a great experience.'

The Mancunian actor was a familiar face on television long before he reached the cobbles of *Coronation Street*. In 1999 he shot to fame as Vince in hard-hitting drama *Queer as Folk* and has since starred in *Hotel Babylon*, *Clocking Off* and the Channel 4 comedy drama *Totally Frank*. Before he became a household name, however, he had a small part in *Titanic*, as wireless operator Harold Bride, and reckons Leonardo DiCaprio still owes him $30 from a poker game.

His latest role is in an ITV drama, *Collision*, in which he and real-life brother Dean Lennox Kelly, of *Shameless* fame, play screen siblings for the first time.

'Working with my brother is a box I've always wanted to tick,' he says.

Since joining *Corrie* in 2008 as knicker factory Underworld's new boss, Craig has had the women falling at his feet – but he's hoping the roles aren't reversed in *Strictly*.

'The biggest fear is to look foolish in front of the nation, to mess up badly. Not knowing how I am going to cope with dancing live until the first live show is terrifying … it's like abseiling without a rope!

'When I got the call to take part in *Strictly Come Dancing*, I was excited and terrified in equal measure. Let me tell you, it's frightening.'

The 38-year-old actor, who married wife Camilla last year, reckons he is a total novice on the dance floor.

'I have absolutely no past experience in dancing – the only dancing I have ever done is after a few beers at a disco,' he says. 'We didn't do a first dance at our wedding; we were going to do a last dance instead, but they shut the venue down before we got round to it.'

According to Craig, wife Camilla is looking forward to him picking up a few tips.

'Last year I watched the series and said it was the only show like this I would appear on. And here I am! It looks like a lot of fun and like a huge,

adventurous challenge and I was a fan of the show for many years. My wife thought that it would be great for future moves on the dance floor!'

While most men look to the likes of Mark Ramprakash and Darren Gough as their series heroes so far, Craig has picked an unusual icon.

'The one that springs to mind is John Sergeant,' he says. 'He had such dignity and grace and such self-deprecating humour. That was brilliant to watch.'

Worried about being 'rubbish in front of half the nation', the soap heartthrob is hoping he'll deal well with the judges' comments.

'I will take it all with a pinch of salt,' he predicts. 'These guys are experts and I am not a great dancer – as long as I try my best and give my all, I will just have to take it on the chin.'

Dancing with Latin supremo Flavia Cacace, Craig reckons ballroom is likely to be his forte.

'If I had to choose I would probably prefer ballroom. I like the elegance and class that is associated with ballroom. It looks like you can play a character and immerse yourself in the role.

'But what I'm most looking forward to is doing the first dance, knowing it went well and having a pint in the bar after. That will be a nice pint!'

Flavia Cacace

Meeting fellow Italian Vincent Simone at Guildford Dance School 13 years ago was the start of a partnership that would see Flavia become a world champion on the tango circuit. Although she was born in Naples, she moved to Surrey when she was four and started dance classes there aged six.

After joining *Strictly* in series four, where she was paired with Jimmy Tarbuck, who unfortunately dropped out due to ill health, she returned in triumphant style to take Matt Di Angelo all the way to the final, where they lost out to Alesha and Matthew. Her bad luck returned for series six, however, when she was knocked out in week one with Phil Daniels.

How was dancing with Matt in series five?

What surprised me the most about Matt is how increasingly hard he tried – he really gave it his all and there is no more you can ask than that. Every single time he gave it 110 per cent. Matt was genuinely devastated when things went wrong, and that happened a few times. He put himself under pressure to do well for me. Making the final alone made me as happy as if we'd won.

What about your other two celeb partners?

What can I say about Jimmy! Our time together was unfortunately very short and not the best of endings, but the time I spent with him I enjoyed; I loved his comments to the judges on the first live show. He was very lovely and protective towards me and tried so hard to please me.

I enjoyed my short time with Phil Daniels and I think he had lots more to offer – such a shame.

Ideal celebrity?

After dancing with a comedian and two actors, I would like to partner a sportsperson. To experience the challenge of working with someone from a sports background would be different and interesting for me.

Favourite dance?

Although I love the tango, my favourite ballroom dance is actually the foxtrot. I love the feeling of gliding across a dance floor to beautiful, sensual music. My favourite Latin dance is the rumba – I love the music and interpreting it through dance in a subtle way.

Hopes for series seven?

The same as each series – to win and to have a memorable experience that I will always remember and cherish.

Any embarrassing moments you'd like to share?

During a signing session after a performance, we were sitting at a table and the guests would join us, sharing our chair to have a picture. I was trying to be nice and leave as much space as possible and misjudged the size of the chair. Almost in slow motion, I fell sideways on to the floor for everyone to see. Smiling was not a problem for the following hour …

Zoe Lucker & James Jordan

Glamorous Zoe has surprised herself and her family by taking on the *Strictly* challenge. Not only does she confess to being 'terrible at dancing', but she has also never had a good experience on the dance floor.

'I'm unable to offer you a happy dance memory,' she reveals. 'I can confirm that the past six years have not seen me dance once. Even at weddings and social events, I'm the one who sticks around on the dinner table whilst all and sundry are up on the dance floor.

'I haven't acted in anything in which I've needed to learn how to dance. I once attended an audition for *Fame*. God knows why! I walked into the room surrounded by all these dancers. Great figures, all supremely confident, they even walked like dancers! I thought that the best way to bluff my way through would be to stand at the back and copy what they did. Trouble was that the choreography moved so quickly that keeping up was impossible. By the time the routine ended I was pulling a completely different shape to everybody else. Needless to add, I didn't get that part!'

The *Footballers' Wives* star, who is engaged to film editor Jim Herbert, has been off work for a year after having baby Lily, and decided the time has come to take a risk.

'My partner was really surprised to learn I wanted to take part but he's now quite proud of the fact I'm getting out of my comfort zone,' she says. 'I don't take enough risks, I play safe, and with *Strictly* I will have to push the boundaries.'

Born in Huddersfield, West Yorkshire, Zoe trained at the Arden School of Acting in Manchester before joining the Hull Truck Theatre. Moving into television, she won small parts in shows like *Doctors, Trial & Retribution, Where the Heart Is* and *Coronation Street* until, in 2002, she landed her breakthrough role in *Footballers' Wives*.

Manipulative, vicious and hugely watchable, the character of Tanya Turner and her increasingly outrageous storylines made Zoe a household name and also saw her sparring with her heroine, *Dynasty* star Joan Collins.

After two years, in a clever twist, the wag became a lag when Tanya was sentenced to five years for drug offences and popped up in sister show *Bad Girls* as the latest inmate of Larkhall Prison.

Zoe is looking forward to spending time with

her old friend, on-screen enemy Laila Rouass.

'Laila and I will support each other because we both get very nervous and get on fantastically well,' says the 35 year old. 'She has a great sense of humour and she is brilliant. As actors we are used to working as an ensemble so the level of competition between us isn't as much as with the professional dancers. Obviously we don't want to go out there and humiliate ourselves completely and fail but we'll definitely be great support for each other so it is really nice to have her here.'

Having been told she was an awful dancer at drama school, Zoe is very apprehensive about meeting partner James Jordan.

'I hope he picks up quite quickly that I'm terrible at dancing and is an understanding and patient person,' she laughs. 'Some discipline will be good for me but I need a good teacher who'll be able to explain all the technical parts of each dance in terms that someone as useless as me can understand.'

Although she is up for the challenge, Zoe admits she will find it hard to tear herself away from Lily, born in September 2008.

'This is my first time back working after having a baby so it's a bit weird,' she says. 'I have turned down all offers of work since she was born, mainly because I've not wanted to be away from my little girl, but when this offer came along I had to rethink. It took me a while definitely to agree because by nature I'm a nervous person and this will test me. I get nervous watching the show on television, for heaven's sake!

'I hope Lily will grow up to feel inspired by what I achieve on *Strictly*.'

And when it comes to choosing the music, Lily is still firmly on her mind.

'I quite fancy the idea of dancing to some big-band sounds – Sinatra, 50s jazz, that kind of thing,' she says. 'My baby girl was born to the Aretha Franklin song "I Say a Little Prayer" so dancing to that particular piece of music on *Strictly* would be lovely.'

James Jordan

Kent-born James started *Strictly Come Dancing* with the curse of the fours. He started in series four, going out in the fourth round with Georgina Bouzova, and history repeated itself in the following series when he had a shock exit in week four with Gabby Logan, despite their excellent scores.

Series six saw the Latin American professional buck the trend with gorgeous actress Cheri Lunghi, who made it to week nine before falling victim to the dance-off.

James started dance classes at the age of 11 and first met wife and dance partner Ola ten years ago. They turned professional in 2003 and taught in Hong Kong for three years before moving back to Kent.

How did you meet Ola?

When I turned 21 I could no longer take part in youth competitions. To be honest, I was fed up with dancing for a while, and just wanted a break. I split with my partner, but earlier on at a competition I had seen Ola dancing and thought she was absolutely amazing even though she was only 15 years old! When I split with my partner I immediately thought of Ola.

I took a six-month break and then decided to travel to Poland and have a try-out with Ola. We were perfect together and within three weeks Ola had moved to the UK and become my dance partner.

How is it working with Ola?

We are exactly the same together at work and at home, and I'm not prepared to change my character for anyone. I won't change my attitude just because we are on television and suddenly competing against each other – I'll be the same with my wife on a Saturday night as I will be on a Monday morning.

Were you upset to go out so soon in series five?

With Gabby I thought, This is my chance to make it to the final. It was a major shock to go out in week four. Gabby was a pleasure to teach, extremely hard working, and it was devastating for her to be out so early.

What is your teaching style?

I'm very straightforward and to the point, pretty patient, and if my pupil doesn't get it, then I'll explain it a few times. But in *Strictly* I haven't got time to explain it too much – we need to move on, so this is where we can clash!

Favourite dance?

The rumba is a very passionate dance and it allows you to get up close and personal with your partner. In ballroom I love the foxtrot. This is the smoothest of the ballroom dances and as I'm a smooth guy it suits me very well.

Hopes for series seven?

After working with Cherie every day during the last series, I wouldn't have changed her for the world. I had the best celebrity. I got past my four-week curse and this year I want the trophy.

Quit while you're ahead could easily be the motto of Camilla Dallerup. After dancing her way to the season-six title, the golden girl hung up her *Strictly* sequins and waltzed off into the sunset, clutching her long-coveted trophy.

'It's the best leaving present I could ask for,' she says. 'I knew all series that this would be my last one so the fact that we got to the final and we won was perfect, like a gift from above.'

Five years before, when *Strictly* first burst on to the screen in an explosion of glitter and glitz, Camilla was one of the original eight dancers.

asked me before the show, "What happens if you guys become celebrities?", and it was quite a wise question but not a thing that any of us thought of really. Everything happened so quickly and on such a big scale but it has been an amazing journey.'

Camilla's first celebrity partner was David Dickinson, who was to be her least successful pupil over the six series, being the second to leave the competition. But the feisty Latin champ loves a challenge.

From there she went from strength to strength, with Roger Black, James Martin, Ray Fearon and Gethin Jones all upping the ante before the final victory with Tom Chambers. With each person came a new challenge – but she has loved dancing with all of her pupils.

'It's funny because when I met Roger Black, he was a competitive person and I thought, He'll do well, but

CAMILLA DALLERUP
Goodbye Girl

She admits that she was initially worried that the programme would ridicule the dance world, as many films and documentaries had in the past, but the producers soon put her mind at ease.

'A few people said, "It will be all about feather boas and fake tan,"' she recalls. 'We sat down with the BBC and asked them whether it would be educational, in that it would help people to understand more about the world of ballroom dancing, the hard work behind it and the technical skills. The BBC said, "Yes, absolutely. That's exactly what we want," so I was thrilled to be part of it. The viewers have learned so much about ballroom dancing so it has been everything they promised and more.'

The first series had its downside for the Danish beauty, who split with dance partner and fiancé Brendan Cole halfway through.

'I was in a bit of turmoil and I went from being completely unknown to the front of the newspapers. It was a bit of a whirlwind. Someone

then it depends how much time they can put in,' she reveals. 'He pulled it out of the bag on the Saturday and he was always able to perform because of his sports mentality.

'But when I met James Martin in series three, I definitely didn't think, Final, here we come, because, bless him, he really couldn't move. But his attitude was, "I know I can't dance but I will do anything you say to improve." He made it to the semi-final because he worked so hard, so he was a wonderful student.'

Disappointment came in series four when actor Ray Fearon was knocked out in week six, despite good scores from the judges.

'Ray Fearon was the best dancer out of all of them but he just didn't get the public vote,' remembers Camilla. 'He really wanted to make it perfect and it's not always perfection that wins, but I really enjoyed dancing with him.'

And she reveals she is still great friends with all her past celeb partners. 'They're

who always wanted to dance. And the song was so appropriate, with my life falling apart and coming together again, so everything came together for that dance. That week, when we practised it every day, we loved it so much!'

The stunning professional, who partners Ian Waite on the dance circuit, says she will miss her weekend whirlwind.

'I'll never forget dancing with Cliff Richard – what an entertainer!' she says. 'We've had quite a few moments, Ian and I, when we've stood in front of the various acts that have been on and looked at each other and said, "This is cool!". I will really miss the Saturday nights because after all that hard work I'm exhausted but the Saturday nights were amazing!'

And while she will be able to skip the intense weeks of training, Camilla says the viewers haven't seen the last of her yet.

'I hope I'll always be involved in Strictly one way or another. I have new challenges ahead but it was such a wonderful time in my life so I'm sure you'll see me again.'

all really different and I am so proud of all of them.

'Gethin found it very natural and he learned very easily but he struggled with the performance. Tom had the performance but struggled with the technical stuff, so if you could blend Tom and Gethin into one, you'd have the perfect dance partner!'

The 35 year old, who has been dancing since she was two and has several Latin American Championships under her sparkly belt, admits that she enjoyed the gamble of the contest.

'There were moments when I thought, Oh my God, what am I going to do? We've got three days to go and none of the choreography is sticking. But I found ways of getting through to the celebrities and ways of teaching them the absolute essentials to make it through.

'When I first met Tom it was pretty magic,' she says. 'We chatted about our vision and what we'd always wanted to do in life and the showdance became what we were dancing for the whole time. I was a dancer who always wanted to be an actress, he was an actor

Laila Rouass
Anton Du Beke

It's stilettos at dawn as *Footballers' Wives* arch enemies Laila and Zoe battle it out once again, this time on the dance floor. The pair played scheming rivals for Premier League star Conrad Gates' affections in the glamorous series and will now compete for the famous glitterball trophy. But off screen they are a million miles from their devious characters and are really good friends.

'Zoe and I are going to support each other,' says Laila. 'I haven't even thought about the competition yet. All I want to do is get through the first week and then it'll be like playtime.'

The 34 year old is a huge fan of the show and has always wanted to take part. Now she is looking forward to months of 'pure pampering'. Has she been watching the right show?

'I was completely addicted to the last two years and used to watch from the comfort of my sofa wishing I was on the other side of the screen, looking as glamorous as all the female dancers!' she chirps. 'This is a dream come true!

'How could any girl turn down a few weeks, possibly months, of pure pampering? Tans, nails, fancy dresses, an opportunity to lose weight … I'd have been foolish to say no!

'Earlier this year I met with my friend Cherie Lunghi, who was so enthusiastic when describing her experience on the show. She told me that I should jump at the opportunity should the invite come my way and that's exactly what I did.'

The exotic beauty, who has a Moroccan father and Indian mother, began modelling at the age of 17 and a year later was cast in a breakthrough role in the film *City of Dreams*, shot in Bombay. After a quick shift from Bollywood to Hollywood, to star alongside Heath Ledger in *The Four Feathers*, she returned to India to present *Close-Up Close Encounters*, the country's version of *Blind Date*.

Back in her home town of London, Laila was cast in soaps *Family Affairs* and *Hollyoaks* before landing the role of superbitch Amber Gates in *Footballers' Wives*.

The stunning actress has since become a mum, discovering she was pregnant after going to the doctor with back pain, and giving birth to daughter Inez in 2007.

As one of seven children, her parents couldn't afford dance classes when she was growing up so she is starting with a clean slate.

'I've never had any formal training,' she says. 'Come to think of it I've only ever danced in social settings – weddings, birthday parties, clubs, etc. In that situation I can dance to just about anything.

'I'm a big Prince fan so any time his music is played at weddings then I'm up on the dance floor. Any cheesy music and I'm up there! I love the Bee Gees and am embarrassed to admit that I'm a big Ricky Martin fan too. I would love to dance to any of those guys.

'I can do a terrible moonwalk but that will not win me many points from your judges.'

Although she has no idea which of the dances she will excel at, she is most worried about the speedier steps.

'I am absolutely dreading the cha cha cha,' she admits. 'That one just seems so fast and technical. Also, thinking about this, the rumba and the quickstep will give me sleepless nights too. I guess I'll just try to have as much fun as possible in those weeks.'

Set to dance with *Strictly*'s funnyman, Anton Du Beke, Laila is modest about her chances of lifting the trophy at the end of the series, saying audiences will have to wait and see.

'I'd absolutely love to win but wouldn't want to say whether or not I can,' she said. 'Come back to me in the first week – I'll know then!

'Whatever happens and however far I go with this thing, I just want to enjoy the journey. I'll remember this experience for the rest of my life. How many times will I receive a crash course in dance from the best teachers in the world?'

Anton Du Beke

The hilarious hoofer hasn't had much luck in the celebrity partners recently, going out after the first dance with Gillian Taylforth in series six, in week five with Jan Ravens in series four and, in between, having to deal with double-left-footer Kate Garraway. His most successful run was in the first series, when he made it to the semi-finals with the elegant Lesley Garrett, so maybe this year it will be his turn to shine.

The busy ballroom star, who started dancing at the age of 14 because of all the girls he could meet at dance class, has partnered *Strictly* star Erin Boag for 11 years. Anton answered a few questions between twirls around the floor.

How was series six for you?

Absolutely lovely but brief! Gillian was marvellous, dedicated and fun and I thought she danced the foxtrot very well. However, it was a very competitive year for the ladies and we went out all too soon!

What's your favourite dance?

My favourite dance is the foxtrot. It's a proper dance with proper music. It has class. Out of the Latin, I can't possibly choose between the paso doble and the rumba, they are both such passionate, strong dances. I much prefer ballroom, though, because I think Latin dancing is a bit of a nonsense, but don't tell the others that! I always loved the tradition and class of the ballroom, which made sense to me.

Who would you like to dance with?

I wouldn't like to be paired with a celebrity who hasn't seen the show and doesn't really understand the work required and my worst fear is working with someone who doesn't think I'm the best dancer in the world!

After having judged *Let's Dance for Comic Relief* I wonder if I should dance with a man as they were so good on that show, although watching Robert Webb turned out to be one of the most unnerving experiences of the year. But I would love to dance with Jo Brand!

How has *Strictly* changed you?

Since being involved in *Strictly Come Dancing*, my life has changed completely. I can't walk down the street without women throwing themselves at me.

Hopes for series seven?

Much the same as virtually every other year – I would love to get to dance all the dances and still be in the show in November and December!

Glitterball Challenge

Choose Latin or ballroom and dance your way to the *Strictly Come Dancing* trophy.

You're the belle of the ball. Go on 7 spaces

3

DANCE OFF

2

1

First-night nerves. Miss a turn

2

1

First-night nerves. Miss a turn

START LATIN

START BALL ROOM

16 FINAL

Sprained ankle. Miss a turn

15

Sprained ankle. Miss a turn

15

Terrible tango. Start again, try Latin

14

You slip in your salsa. Miss a turn

14

13

DANCE OFF

12

13

Dull, dull, dull. Start again with ballroom

12

How to play
For 2–4 players

The object of the game is to get from your first dance in week one to the final, and to lift the glittering prize.

You'll need a dice and some counters or coins.

Choose between the Latin or ballroom dances and throw a six to start.

If you land on a Dance-Off square, you and the player to your left must both throw the dice and the player with the highest score moves on that number of squares.

Once you're through to the final, you must score the exact number needed to land on the trophy and become the *Strictly Come Dancing* champion.

Good luck – and keep dancing!

Phil Tufnell
Katya Virshilas

Cheeky chappie Phil ate bush tucker and overcame his fears to be crowned King of the Jungle in *I'm a Celebrity* ... and faced tough questions as team captain on *A Question of Sport*, but neither roles have prepared him for this latest ordeal. And it isn't the dancing that's worrying him.

'I'm slightly nervous about those costumes,' he admits. 'Crikey! I've no idea what I'll look like in something sequined, glitzy and glamorous. I only slip into a black tie every now and again for awards shows. I'm not a particularly glitzy kind of guy.

'I hope that I'm not put into anything sleeveless or a leotard for show one. I hope that with regards to the costumes I'm led into things gently.'

The former cricketer and presenter of *The One Show* has seen plenty of his colleagues go through the show, including his *A Question of Sport* rival Matt Dawson and his fellow England batsmen.

'Last year, I loved it and I'd come down to support Christine [Bleakley],' he says. 'She works with me on *The One Show* and so I had to offer my support. I watched when Ramps [Mark Ramprakash] and Goughie [Darren Gough] featured. I came down to see the show then and was impressed by Ramps's dance. Good stuff!

'Cricketers always seem to do well on the show. I'll no doubt become known as the only cricketer who couldn't dance on *Strictly*!'

The saucy spin-bowler began his career in 1986 when he made his debut with Middlesex, with whom he played for 20 years, gaining 1000 first-class wickets, a remarkable feat achieved by only three other Englishmen. In 1990, he was chosen to represent England in a Test match at the Melbourne Cricket Ground on the Ashes tour of Australia and seven years on he helped England to an Ashes victory at the Oval when he took 11 wickets for 93 runs.

When he signed up for *Strictly*, no one was more surprised than his wife Dawn.

'When my wife found out she said, "God, Phil, what have you done?"' he laughs. 'She's not the biggest fan of my dancing. Well, you're only young once, aren't you? It's a really exciting show and the chance to take part was a really exciting opportunity for me.'

But he admits his previous dancing experience is negligible, and usually involves a few drinks.

'The last time I danced was a while back,' he confesses. 'There were a few beers involved, no doubt! I've been known to stagger around on a

dance floor at a birthday party but I'm not sure that anybody would call what I do dancing.

'My wife isn't too impressed with my moves. She would give me five out of ten and that's her being generous. It'll be interesting to see how much support she gives me this year. When I dance at parties she'll usually be the one to tell me to sit down.'

But being a sportsman, Phil is ready to give it his all and take whatever flak he gets from the fearsome foursome.

'Those judges? Blimey! You know what? I'll just take on board everything that they have to say. I'll take it on the chin.

'I'll stand there, ears open. If they say I'm a bad dancer then I must have been rubbish and will try and get better.

'I'm a sportsman and have been dealing with criticism all my life so I'm used to people not painting me in a positive light. There'll be no tears.'

The 43-year-old star is most worried about getting through the first dance.

'I think my main fear will come on the first night when I'm stood backstage and my name is announced,' he says. 'Hmm … Can imagine the heart will be pounding and I'll be feeling ever so slightly ticklish at that moment!'

And Phil, who will be dancing with talented newcomer Katya Virshilas, has one final wish.

'My main hope is that I'm partnered with somebody who's a far better dancer than me!'

Katya Virshilas

Lovely Lithuanian Katya started dancing aged six after her family moved to Israel. Seven years later they moved to Vancouver, Canada, and Katya discovered ballroom.

'I remember watching Tony Meredith and Melanie LaPatin [four-time North American Latin Champions] in a competition. Melanie was wearing this beautiful sequined gown – the glamour took my breath away,' she says. After she was enrolled in a class, the 13 year old was upset when the instructor told her she was too old and would never achieve anything, so she refused to return. However, a $50 bribe from her mum changed her mind and she set out to prove the teacher wrong.

Three years later she became the youngest-ever British Columbian Latin Dance Champion at the age of 16 and in 2000 she won the Canadian Latin Championship, earning a place at the World Championships representing Canada in St Petersburg, Russia.

As her dance career developed she also explored acting and landed herself a role in the 2003 film *Shall We Dance?* And she's no stranger to training celebrities, having tutored the film's stars, Richard Gere and Jennifer Lopez, backstage!

She went on to star in *Take the Lead*, in which she co-choreographed, trained and danced in an iconic tango scene with Antonio Banderas. As a result, top Bollywood choreographer Shiamak Davar invited her to India to teach Latin dance workshops and she also performed in his stage production, *I Believe*, in front of more than 60,000 spectators.

Katya is trained in ballroom, Latin, jazz, ballet, hip-hop, modern, folk dance, Broadway jazz, burlesque, swing, mambo and salsa.

Favourite ballroom dance?
It's the tango music that I connect with the most. When I hear it I feel like I can do and conquer anything.

Favourite Latin American dance?
The rumba because it is full of raw emotion and is beautifully feminine. Its slow, drawn-out movement expresses endless emotion.

Approach to teaching?
Teaching children and teens has always been important to me and it is a necessity in my life. As I am still young the children relate to me and I love to show them the cool side of ballroom dancing.

Teaching a celeb?
I think many celebrities are inhibited by having to reveal their weaknesses. Being a great celebrity teacher is about building trust, cultivating their dancing talent and letting them shine. I hope that my celebrity will be able to match my eagerness constantly to try fresh approaches to dancing.

What are you looking forward to most?
Of course I'm looking forward to dancing the most, with the other pros as well as my celebrity. I'm also excited to show people how original and inspiring ballroom can be.

Strictly stylist Su Judd always has her work cut out with the quick turnaround of costumes. And while there was an abundance of tall, elegant ladies to deck out in fabulous frocks, the team also had to deal with a portly presenter whose waistband shrunk every week, a six-foot-six swimmer with perfect pecs and a rugby player with bulging biceps.

But it wasn't just the boys wearing the trousers in the last series. A new ruling on the dress code meant that the girls could too, and professional Ola Jordan took full advantage with a skin-tight animal print catsuit that caused quite a stir in week one.

'Every time she walked down the stairs in it, the whole arena gasped, so we knew it was a winner. I think she looked amazing.'

Strictly Style

It's a tough job but someone's got to do it – and Su is not complaining one bit.

'They were a really good team of boys this year,' she reveals. 'Having sportsmen in the team always brings on a sort of locker-room mentality. There's a lot of one-upmanship but I can use that.'

'Austin wanted to show his muscles off but we tried to keep them in as much as possible because it's much better for the line when they're dancing. Every other week he would come in and say, "Can I cut the sleeves off?" and we'd have a bit of a laugh about it.'

Another favourite was god-like Olympic champ Mark Foster, who turned out to be a very gentle giant.

'He was the easiest celebrity I've ever had to dress,' recalls Su. 'The first time we met, at the photo shoot, I asked, "Would you go bare chested?" and he said, "Yeah, if you want me to." We gave him a little bolero jacket because we thought we'd better retain a little bit of mystery but he would happily have done it naked!'

Winning celeb Tom Chambers may not have had Austin's biceps and Mark's pecs, but he made up for it with another part of his anatomy, according to Su.

'Tom is slim and more of a Fred Astaire build than the others,' she says. 'His bottom was a lovely pert bottom, so he instantly looked good in Latin trousers!'

When it came to getting fit, John Sergeant amazed everybody by dancing his way into a different body.

'John lost a colossal amount of weight,' she says. 'It really was astonishing, to lose 2 stone in three months, and his trousers came in every week.'

RACHEL'S RUMBA DRESS

This was an 'attitude-changing' rumba dress so it's my favourite outfit of the series. The week before she'd almost been out after dancing the American smooth and when she came in for a meeting I told her she had to stop playing it safe. She had been nervous about letting too much show.

The dress had already been made for Ola and, when she first tried it on, it was a different shape and in tiger print! It was a feat just to get her into that.

She is a really shy and gentle girl, not at all the pop star you might think, and I think that dress brought about a complete change in her. Her performance in the rumba was really extraordinary.

From that moment Rachel danced with passion and fire – and we take a lot of credit in the costume department for that!

CHERIE'S RUMBA DRESS

It's unusual for people to love the rumba dresses but it was one of those extraordinary weeks where everything just comes right. Rachel's was a new design that was very outré in the dancing world whereas Cherie's was a classic – very high cut on one leg, very long on the other so that she had complete movement.

The dress was white with a black belt and black bars across nude panelling down one side, so it looked as if it showed flesh but it didn't. It was one shoulder, which was very in that year, and we gave her the long angel-skin white glove, which is slightly see-through.

Cherie was the ideal body to dress. She was a perfect size ten, wasn't afraid of showing anything and there was nothing we needed to cover up. She really was so classy.

LISA SNOWDON'S CHA CHA CHA DRESS

For her first cha cha cha, Lisa wore an orange fringed dress that graduated into pink. When she repeated the dance for the final, she was supposed to wear a copy in silver going down to purple, which was made and ready to be worn, but she loved the original so much that she asked me if she could wear the orange dress again. Of course, I said, 'If it will help you win, then yes!'

Lisa has a lovely figure but because she is rather well endowed on top it was trickier to design dresses for her that had enough support but still looked great. She has the most amazing long spine so we tried to give her an open back as much as possible, but very often ended up putting a back strap on.

I loved the whole process with her. From the beginning, she was really active and getting involved. She is well aware of what works well with her.

HEATHER'S VIENNESE WALTZ DRESS

Heather had some fantastic dresses. Her Viennese waltz was a fairytale full-skirted, passion-pink ballgown but it was actually made to look like one of those covers you put over a toilet roll in the seventies!

The viewer never saw that, of course, because we put a layer of silk over the top. Underneath that was many hours of work, and numerous frills, to give the skirt its princess fullness without using tulle. Heather is tiny but she has a great figure, with a tiny waist and great boobs.

KRISTINA'S FAREWELL WALTZ

I wouldn't usually include a professional's dress in my top picks but this had special significance for all of us.

It was a pale gold in a very elegant, simple shape. We had to make it in a couple of days because her partner, John Sergeant, quit on Wednesday and it had to be ready by Friday. We wanted to give her the full princess skirt, to make her look as romantic and elegant as possible, so that she and John could bow out in style. This dress showed off her amazing body and gave her the perfect Marilyn Monroe moment.

TOM'S SAMBA SHIRT

The starburst, or fireworks, sequined shirt that Tom wore for his samba was something that I had bought on a whim. We had made him a white shirt with ruffles to go with Camilla's lovely white, blousy dress, which was very seventies and based on *Saturday Night Fever*. Then I saw this shirt hanging up in one of the costumiers and, although it's actually designed for a young boy, I brought it in with me.

Tom had embraced the whole thing from day one – he was the first to wear a satin shirt, he was happy to wear see-through shirts – and he was getting braver each week. When I produced this shirt everyone was laughing at me, saying, 'You can't put that on screen!' But when it was on screen, under the lights, it was spectacular. He was perfect for it because he was like a young, bouncy puppy and you could do what you wanted with him.

Tom and Camilla were a great couple because they got on so well, he trusted us and her, and he got on and did it.

Ricky Whittle
Natalie Lowe

Give him a tight-fitting Austin Healey-type Latin shirt and *Hollyoaks* hunk Ricky is bound to get the teenage girls on his side.

The former model, famous for his toned torso and numerous 'Sexiest Male' soap awards, is prepared to go as far as necessary to clinch that trophy and his strategy is guaranteed to raise votes – and temperatures.

'I love all the sexy Latin stuff – the salsa, the rumba,' he confesses. 'I get flustered in suits, so if I'm in something else it would be better. To be honest if it gets me through to the final I'll dance in my thong!'

The Oldham-born actor is the son of an RAF officer, whose career meant numerous moves around the world. A keen sportsman, Ricky was on course to becoming a professional footballer when his dreams were dashed by injury, so he decided to study law at Southampton University. While there he was offered modelling deals and, in 2002, applied to star in Sky One's *Dream Team*. Having landed a role, he decided to forfeit life in the courtroom for one in front of the camera, and in 2006 he was cast as bad boy Calvin Valentine in *Hollyoaks*.

Although he has had no training, Ricky does like to dance in his spare time, especially with girlfriend and co-star Carley Stenson, who plays Steph Cunningham.

'I dance all the time and when my girlfriend and I go on holiday we try and do the *Dirty Dancing* lift,' he laughs. 'Our friends got married last Saturday so we also danced then.

'I once had to dance to "Footloose", for *Let's Dance for Comic Relief*. I enjoy a bit of a boogie in a club. As soon as a tune begins that you like you just can't help bobbing your head.'

And it was purely his love of dancing that brought him to the show.

'*Strictly Come Dancing* is the only show that I would do – I love dancing,' he says. 'When I was growing up I hung out with the girls, instead of playing computer games with the boys, and went clubbing and dancing with them.

'I appreciate all sorts of dance and the chance to learn a new skill is too good to miss. I was an even bigger fan of *Come Dancing* back in the day, before any celebrities started taking part!'

In his ponderings on the *Strictly* sensation, Ricky has come up with an unusual angle – sympathy for the judges.

'There were great dances last year,' he explains. 'When you see people improve so much it is amazing, like Lisa Snowdon – it must be so hard for the judges. Would you rather vote for someone who has been consistently good, or vote for someone who has made such a huge improvement?'

Ricky's biggest fear is going out in week one and letting his new partner, *Strictly* novice Natalie Lowe, down.

'I want to win. I love competitive sports and so anything I get involved in I want to win. To go out in week one would be catastrophic. I want to do my partner justice. I want to learn loads of dances and I would definitely like to get to the final.

'I have got so many people hoping to come and watch the show – so I can't go out early in the series otherwise they will not get the chance to come and see me dance.'

Natalie Lowe

This may be her first series in the UK, but Natalie has already triumphed in the Australian version, winning one series of *Dancing with the Stars*, with Aussie footballer Anthony Koutoufides, and coming second in two other series.

Born in Sydney, the ballroom specialist knew she wanted to be a dancer long before she was allowed to start classes. 'For two years I watched my elder brother Glenn and sister Kylie dance. It was only a matter of time before I put on my first pair of dancing shoes.'

At eight she and her dance partner were already representing her country and winning championships, including South Pacific, New South Wales, Victorian and Queensland Open and Australasian in New Zealand. As a teenager she began to dance with brother Glenn who was already competing on the adult circuit. They were preparing to move to Europe when a family illness prevented them, but fate intervened and she was picked as a regular on *Dancing with the Stars*.

Favourite ballroom dance?

To see a great couple dance a waltz can be truly mesmerising. It is a dance of grace, elegance and beauty, it takes you away from reality and is most fulfilling to dance.

Favourite Latin American dance?

The rumba is the one dance that has the ability to showcase a lot of different emotions and with beautiful technique it really makes you appreciate the strength and tone of a Latin dancer.

What was *Dancing with the Stars* like?

Dancing with the Stars has changed my life. Over the past four years I have met the most wonderful people.

I feel most alive when I am on the show. You just can't beat the adrenalin and excitement that a live show brings. I really like dancing with a live band, the rehearsals leading up to the performance and most of all the weeks of training with your new dance partner.

Approach to teaching?

I like to teach a few basic fundamentals then get the routine finished – then revisit technique and polish choreography. Patience is the key, keep it fun … but know that it has to be quality rehearsal time.

Ideal celeb?

Someone who is genuine, outgoing and willing to put in the hours, someone who is eager to learn and will be as passionate about the journey as I am. I have worked with sportsmen in Australia and they know what hard work is, they are disciplined and I like the competitive edge that comes out in them during the dance competition. Actors are also good. A born entertainer is really quite easy to mould because *Strictly Come Dancing* is all about confidence, connection and entertainment.

What are you most looking forward to on *SCD*?

I love nothing more than to teach someone to dance from scratch. For me there is nothing more rewarding than seeing the progress in the celebrity from one week to the next, the day they lead you properly instead of you leading them – all those little things just make the experience more valuable.

When *Strictly* hit the road in the wake of the last series, it boasted a host of spectacular talent – and Bruno Tonioli (only joking, Bruno!).

The series-six winner and runner-up, Tom Chambers and Rachel Stevens, were dancing with their original partners so Camilla Dallerup, not being able to be in two places at one time, had to relinquish her rights to salsa stud Gethin Jones to Flavia Cacace. Jodie Kidd and Ian

as she was on the show. Tom was very good, and Jill Halfpenny was there still doing that brilliant jive. I said before, "On the sixth series of *Strictly Come Dancing* one jive stands out as the best there's ever been and that was Jill Halfpenny's," and I'm still of that opinion. The routine was amazing. That probably got more tens from the judges than any other dance on tour.'

However, the name on everybody's lips when talking about the tour, though not necessarily for his hoofing ability, was Julian Clary.

'Julian Clary is beyond genius,' gushes Arlene. 'The wit, the smart, the brains ... words pour out of his mouth like liquid – it's endless but hilarious. I only had to look round at the screen and I

What Goes On Tour...

The inside info on Strictly Come Dancing Live

Waite joined the party and Cherie Lunghi was reunited with James Jordan, while his wife Ola got together with series-five partner Kenny Logan. Series-two star Julian Clary danced with the lovely Lilia Kopylova in the absence of Erin Boag and jivin' Jill Halfpenny returned to the *Strictly* fold to relive her time with Darren Bennett.

Rachel may have been pipped at the post by Tom on the series final, but she more than made up for it on tour, winning 26 times out of 40!

'Rachel and Vincent came into their own,' comments Arlene. 'They were constantly practising and working and for someone who had already done well in the competition to go on working, striving and rehearsing to improve was amazing. Also James and Cherie were outstanding, incredible to watch.'

With five weeks, eight venues and 40 dates, each of the celebs got their chance to shine and each impressed the judges in different ways.

'Gethin Jones was incredible,' recalls Len. 'Gethin was a wonderful dancer. Cherie Lunghi was so beautiful,

would be laughing, night after night.'

Craig reveals that the cunning comedian had a few tricks up his sleeve to win the audience over and even managed to win the show on three occasions.

'He used to beg the audience and used the most outrageous ruses, saying he was from the area, his mother was ill and he'd never won anything in his life, ever! When he did win he made this horrendously long speech. "I'd like to thank wardrobe, I'd like to thank Swarovski crystals, the team behind me, catering, I'd like to thank my agent, Lilia's agent, I'd like to thank the band ..." Then he named them all. Then he would end on, "But ultimately, I'd like to thank Kate Winslet." He was hilarious and Lilia was the greatest sport – they were quite a double act.'

Len agrees, calling Julian 'the star of the show' and saying, 'He was so much fun, so he absolutely shook me rigid!'

But while Rachel, Tom and the others wowed them on the dance floor, and Julian had them all in stitches, one man impressed the judges for entirely different reasons.

'Kenny Logan was the heart and soul of the company,' recalls Bruno. 'I'm telling you, everybody should get the chance to work with Kenny Logan. What a team player!

'He kept everyone going, always cheerful, always happy, always funny and everybody fell in love with Kenny. Fabulous fun on stage but as a person, he was the heart of the tour.'

'I enjoyed it this year,' recalls Arlene. 'I felt this year there was a strong bond between us all and it felt like collectively we were all on tour – the dancers, the judges, the celebrities all felt like a group. That had a lot to do with Kenny Logan, who for me is one of the warmest, kindest, most generous-hearted people you could wish to meet.'

Kenny's kilted paso remains one of the most memorable dances in *Strictly* history and, while he failed to win anywhere else, it went down a treat in Glasgow where the patriotic Scots put him and Ola in the top spot at all six shows.

'The scoring system was different this time,' explains Len. 'The judges marked on tour but our marks didn't count – it was purely down to the audience vote. We could say "That was terrible" and give it a six, but it made no odds. So when Kenny did his paso doble in the kilt in Scotland, he won it every time!'

Kate Thornton stepped up to the mark to present the show for the second year running and Len would definitely give her a perfect ten for her performance. 'Kate does a fabulous job on that show. She's a lovely girl and it's not easy because she does both Bruce's and Tess's job and keeps it fresh every night.'

For Bruno, the 2009 tour was his first as he missed the live shows the year before due to TV commitments. He admits that playing in front of up to 18,000 people in an arena was an eye-opener.

'It was absolutely amazing,' he says. 'What I found

was how loyal our fans are. We packed arenas every night – 280,000 people came to see it in four weeks, which was incredible.

'You are not really aware of the popularity of the show until you go out in the country and you have the public there watching you, so you get an immediate reaction, which is absolutely incredible.

'I got a lot of laughs, I must say. Personally I was quite shocked how the public reacted to me because you only get a little bit of that in the studio but it's not as tangible. And they do understand me – despite what Brucie says! They got all the punchlines.

'To see how people receive you is an incredible adrenalin rush. I felt like a member of the Rolling Stones!'

And Craig reveals a new twist to the live shows this year – with the audience biting back.

'The tour has really brought home the catchphrases we all have,' he laughs. 'On tour, I would say, "I have one word for it and it starts with F," and 16,000 people would say "Fab-U-Lous!" I nearly died the first time that happened. Oh, the power of television. It's bizarre.

'Len's "Se-VEN" is always a winner too. Len brought the house down on tour with that score, because he always saved it till last – for Julian Clary. Normally, a seven would get a boo but everyone loves it now.'

The performers were having a great time too, as Tom Chambers reveals: 'The tour was a complete and utter barrel of fun and laughter because it was totally different. It was very relaxed and enjoyable and it was really about giving it back to the public, all the people who supported us through the show. It was wonderful to be able to entertain them in the flesh.'

Tour Table

	Wins	Runner-up
Rachel Stevens and Vincent Simone	26	14
Gethin Jones and Flavia Cacace	6	6
Kenny Logan and Ola Jordan	6	0
Julian Clary and Lilia Kopylova	3	13
Jill Halfpenny and Darren Bennett	3	9
Tom Chambers and Camilla Dallerup	1	2
Cherie Lunghi and James Jordan	0	1
Jodie Kidd and Ian Waite	0	0

Rav Wilding
Aliona Vilani

Crimewatch presenter Rav is bound to be an arresting sight in the tight Latin outfits. The former policeman, who has become something of a pin-up since turning his attention to TV, used to be in the army and reckons his pumped-up physique, developed through years of training, could be useful.

'I think I might be able to do the lifting involved in the Latin dancing so I think I would be better at that,' he predicts. 'However, my past experience in the army has meant that I have done a lot of drill in the parade ground, and drill is all about posture and making it look effortless and natural, so in that respect maybe I would be more suited to the ballroom discipline. Therefore, ballroom might suit me better because it is more relevant to my past.'

The 30 year old, who plays rugby in his spare time, is worried the costumes may be too skimpy for his bulging muscles.

'I've got massive thighs and have already burst out of three suits,' he laughs. 'My thighs are 27 inches in circumference and I'm worried about a wardrobe malfunction on *Strictly Come Dancing*. I'm worried that if something rips on the dance floor the viewers might see a little more than they anticipated.

'As manly as I am, I thought Vincent and Flavia's Argentine tango was absolutely amazing and I would love to be able to pull something like that off by the end of the series, but I am fearful that there are so many moves to remember that I will just forget the routine halfway through.'

Born in Canterbury, Kent, Rav is the second of five children by a Mauritian father and English mother, both nurses. At 17 he joined the British army but his career was cut short four years later when he broke his leg during a training run. From there he joined the Metropolitan police, where he was involved in the tragic Damilola Taylor case. He was then part of a specialist unit dedicated to working on the tough estate where the ten year old died.

After two years in the Met, Rav applied for a Channel 4 reality show that would follow contestants living in an Australian rainforest for three months and was chosen from 50,000 applicants. After his spell in the show, named *Eden*, he returned to policing and was promoted to the rank of detective constable.

'Working for the Met in London, I've probably encountered more things in eight years than some policemen get in a lifetime,' he says. 'I've had knives pulled on me, but the scariest moment was when I was holding someone's head after they'd been shot at point-blank range. I needed to stay and help the man, but at the same time there was a real risk the gunman might come back and finish us off. Things like that could stay with you for life if you let them, but I'm a pretty strong character.'

After numerous interviews and presenter courses, Rav was offered the chance to front *Crimewatch* in 2004 and women switched on the programme in their droves. But he and girlfriend Lauren laugh off his heartthrob status.

'It's a bit silly really,' he says. 'I don't think too much about it. Friends say there are fansites on the web about me, but I don't pay much attention. It's flattering, but my feet are on the ground.'

Despite the many frightening things he has faced in the force, Rav is quaking in his dancing shoes over the Saturday-night routines with newcomer Aliona Vilani.

'As a viewer I thought the last series of *Strictly Come Dancing* was fantastic, but as a contestant I am now terrified, because watching them dance last year, they were so brilliant.

'I have absolutely no dance experience whatsoever. I don't drink anymore so I can't even claim to have drunkenly staggered on to a dance floor in recent years. Alcohol brings with it the confidence to get up and boogie when there's music on but because I don't drink I haven't even done that. Because of this, I am so nervous about taking part.'

And while he says he can take a pounding from the judges, *Strictly* fans who see him outside the studio would be ill-advised to criticise.

'If criticism is constructive and comes from someone who genuinely knows what they are talking about, with 30 or 40 years' experience, then I can deal with it,' he promises. 'If, however, someone were to come up to me in the street and say that I was a rubbish dancer, with no experience themselves, I'd think, Who are you to judge me? You can't dance!'

Aliona Vilani

Exotic beauty Aliona is set to light up the dance floor as one of the new dancers on *Strictly* this year. The 25 year old, who was born and raised in Russia, is a Ten Dance and Latin Champion who describes herself 'as the pussycat of the ballroom world!'.

Aliona started dancing at the age of five when she joined the Arts Gymnasium for classical ballet and performing arts. At 11, she took up ballroom and was soon gracing the finals in Eastern European competitions. She was invited to go to the United States to join the Kaiser Dance Academy, New York, and the entire family moved to the States with her when she was 13. Here she learned salsa, hip-hop and jazz in the prestigious Broadway Dance Center and in 2000 she became a US National Champion in Ten Dance in the Youth category. In 2001 she was chosen as part of the US Amateur Ballroom team. At 16, she began to teach and at 17 turned professional, making her the youngest professional dancer in the US.

Favourite ballroom dance?

Each dance has this certain something special. It's almost like having secrets for yourself in each dance that you let the people in on for a moment when you're performing. I would have to say my favourite is the waltz, because it just takes you into this special dreamy wonderland where you can get away from your everyday life.

Favourite Latin American dance?

My favourite Latin dance is the cha cha cha because I feel that this dance has a lot of different sides to it. I like that it can have all the little characteristics of all the other Latin dances. Cha cha cha in itself is a very cheeky and flirtatious dance and also could have the party feel of samba, the elegance of rumba, arrogance of paso doble and rock 'n' roll feel of jive.

Approach to teaching?

Being a teacher myself has been a major part of my life since I was 16. My parents moved to Florida and I stayed in New York after I finished high school so teaching both adults and children was my main income at the time. When I wasn't competing or dancing in shows I would teach up to 12 hours a day.

I'm very supportive of my students and always make sure that while they're having a good time they are advancing and pushing their limits. It's always rewarding for me to see my students do a great job and if things don't go as well then it's even more rewarding to see them pull through.

Looking forward to teaching a celebrity?

I think that will be something I will find very exciting because there is nothing more satisfying and rewarding than taking an untrained artist and watching them blossom under my wing.

Ideal celeb?

I would love to get someone who will be able to follow my innovative ideas – and keep up with me. My perfect partner would be someone who is physically prepared to take challenges.

Hopes for series seven?

For me, dancing is like having secrets that I can share with the audience. I want to melt people's hearts and take them on a journey. I love to meet new people, to teach new students and just dance my little butt off!

The Strictly League

Every year records are broken and higher scores for each dance are notched up. In series six Lisa Snowdon and Brendan Cole managed to attain the unbeatable score of 80 out of 80 for their two final dances, and Rachel landed a record hat-trick of top scores for different dances. Despite the feast of 40s lapped up in the final weeks, one or two records from previous series were left standing.

At the other end of the scale, Fiona Phillips proudly retains the record for the lowest scores ever and, surprisingly, John Sergeant failed to break any records for bottom scores, although he did tie with the hapless TV presenter on the foxtrot. Just so you can see what the contestants in series seven have to live up to, we bring you the *Strictly* league tables.

Most Perfect Scores

Lisa Snowdon and Brendan Cole:
most 40s scored – 3
Darren Gough and Lilia Kopylova:
most 40s in the Christmas specials – 2
Rachel Stevens and Vincent Simone:
greatest number of tens – 28

Lowest Scores Awarded

Quentin Willson and Hazel Newberry: cha cha cha – 8
Fiona Phillips and Brendan Cole: waltz – 11
Diarmuid Gavin and Nicole Cutler: cha cha cha – 12
Diarmuid Gavin and Nicole Cutler: quickstep – 12
John Sergeant and Kristina Rihanoff: cha cha cha – 12

Best and Worst Dances

Cha cha cha

Best: Lisa Snowdon and Brendan Cole
(series six) **40**
Worst: Quentin Willson
and Hazel Newberry
(series two) **8**

Jive

Best: Jill Halfpenny and Darren Bennett
(series two) **40**
Worst: Fiona Phillips and
Brendan Cole (series three) **8**

Rumba

Best: Matt Di Angelo and Flavia
Cacace (series five); Rachel Stevens and Vincent
Simone (series six) **39**
Worst: Fiona Phillips and Brendan Cole
(series three) **13**

Paso doble

Best: Austin Healey and Erin Boag
(series six) **38**
Worst: Christopher Parker and Hanna Karttunen
(series one); Dennis Taylor and Izabela Hannah
(series three) **15**

Samba

Best: Zoe Ball and Ian Waite (series three) 38

Worst: Christopher Parker and Hanna Karttunen (series one) 15

Waltz

Best: Matt Di Angelo and Flavia Cacace (series five); Gethin Jones and Camilla Dallerup (Christmas special) 40

Worst: Fiona Phillips and Brendan Cole (series three) 11

Quickstep

Best: Darren Gough and Lilia Kopylova (Christmas special); Colin Jackson and Erin Boag (Christmas special); Lisa Snowdon and Brendan Cole (series six) 40

Worst: Diarmuid Gavin and Nicole Cutler (series two) 12

Foxtrot

Best: Rachel Stevens and Vincent Simone (series six); Lisa Snowdon and Brendan Cole (series six) 40

Worst: Fiona Phillips and Brendan Cole (series three); John Sergeant and Kristina Rihanoff (series six) 20

Tango

Best: Rachel Stevens and Vincent Simone (series six) 39

Worst: Diarmuid Gavin and Nicole Cutler (series two) 14

Viennese waltz

Best: Alesha Dixon and Matthew Cutler (series five) 39

Worst: Will Thorp and Hanna Haarala (series three) 23

American smooth

Best: Darren Gough and Lilia Kopylova (Christmas special) 40

Worst: Andrew Castle and Ola Jordan (series six) 14

Salsa

Best: Mark Ramprakash and Karen Hardy (series four) 40

Worst: Kate Garraway and Anton Du Beke (series five) 18

Argentine tango

Best: Mark Ramprakash and Karen Hardy (series four); Rachel Stevens and Vincent Simone (series six) 39

Worst: Matt Dawson and Lilia Kopylova (series four) 30

Jo Wood
Brendan Cole

She may be a granny of six but Jo still rocks. Having been married to one of the most famous faces in rock music for 30 years, the model turned businesswoman still likes to hit the clubs when she gets the chance.

'Nowadays I love going out with my friends for a boogie,' she says. 'I do that a lot.'

I like all the modern artists, like Lady GaGa and Kings of Leon. Those guys produce tunes that I enjoy a boogie to.'

Having travelled all over the world as a model and touring with former husband Ronnie Wood's legendary band the Rolling Stones, she feels a natural affinity for the Latin dances.

'The Latin will be fun, I imagine. All that wonderful rhythm. I've been to Argentina many times and adore watching the flamenco. Those girls are simply divine.

'I did once take part in a South American carnival, probably in Brazil. I was wearing the tiniest outfit and didn't quite know what to do. I asked the girl who was dancing on the next float just what I should do. She said, "Don't think, girl. Just move!" so I did!

'Off I went, twirling around and around. I did that for an hour or so and was so very tired afterwards. Boiling hot too. Looked like a tomato!'

Essex-born Jo, who attended a local convent school until the age of 16, landed herself a modelling contract after becoming the *Sun*'s 'Face of 1972'. After giving birth to son Jamie at 18, she continued her successful modelling career until, aged 22, she met rock star Ronnie and married him. After daughter Leah was born, Jo and her children spent their lives on the road, touring with the Stones while she looked after her husband's wardrobe, diary and diet.

In 1989, after a serious illness made her re-examine her lifestyle, Jo turned to organic living and, disappointed with the lack of beauty products available, launched her own range of organic bath and body-care products. In 2007, her first book, *Naturally: How to Look and Feel Healthy, Energetic and Radiant the Organic Way*, was published.

Undoubtedly fit for her 54 years, the ex-model has a lot to learn to impress on the dance floor.

'I've never had any formal training. Well, I did

attend ballet school many, many, many years ago. I must have been six and I only stuck around in that class for a few weeks. I dropped out because I didn't enjoy myself. I can't remember that much of the training!

'I went to an all-girls school and did have the occasional dance lesson whilst there. But of course my partner would always be a girl so there was never any fun to be had. I remember waltzing on one occasion, just going round and round the sports hall, endlessly!'

The only person more excited than Jo when she landed a place on the show was her mum, the show's number-one fan.

'My mum is the most enormous fan and she kept me up to date with what was going on with the show last year,' says Jo. 'She adores dancing and is so excited about this year.

'She'll call me up every now and again to tell me the show is being repeated on some digital channel and I should tune in quickly!'

Although she is dancing with series-one winner Brendan Cole, she is already pals with another of the professionals.

'I'm good friends with [party organiser] Fran Cutler, who introduced me to her cousin Matthew Cutler a while back. It will be fun when he finds out I'm dancing on his show this year!'

And she is hoping to make many new friends on *Strictly* having watched the backstage camaraderie of previous series.

'Everybody on the show looks as if they have such a happy and enjoyable time, whether they're on that dance floor or chatting with each other backstage,' she says. 'I'm really looking forward to being involved!'

Brendan Cole

Hot-blooded hoofer Brendan was the first professional to win on *Strictly*, after impressing the judges and the public with reluctant ballroom queen Natasha Kaplinsky.

Growing up in a family of dancers, Brendan, his sister and brother once occupied the fifth, second and first ranking in his native New Zealand and, in typically competitive style, he maintains his own position would have been higher were it not for the inexperience of his partners at the time!

After walking away with the trophy in series one, Brendan's luck changed for the next two runs, with Sarah Manners and Fiona Phillips. After being knocked out in week eight with Claire King, things started to look up with Kelly Brook until, sadly, she had to drop out due to a family bereavement.

In series six Brendan looked like hitting the jackpot when he and Lisa began to ring up the perfect scores but, in fact, they finished third.

Favourite dance?
The foxtrot because it is a calm, smooth, sexy dance. It just oozes class. In Latin, the rumba is great because it gives you time to create chemistry with the dance and your partner. It's definitely a dance that has a lot of chemistry.

How was series six for you?
Lisa was a great dancer, a great friend and the kind of partner that a boy wants for *Strictly Come Dancing*. I was very lucky to be partnered with her and apart from the nerves and the occasional tears (OK, a few more than occasional), she was b****y great!

Do you enjoy switching sides to judge on the New Zealand version?
It's a great chance to go home and see my family. I also do the odd demonstration spot on the show, which is nice, as when I left New Zealand 14 years

ago to dance I'm sure many people laughed. Nobody knew what this dancing lark was all about but now with dancing being so popular thanks to the show, it's nice to demonstrate what I've done with it all.

Ideal celeb?
Popular, with stage training, musical, gorgeous, small in stature (for the illegal lifts, of course), driven, happy, competitive, elegant, eloquent, lovely, loves the show and doesn't mind being partnered with me … Yes, I know, it's never going to happen, is it? With Kelly, our partnership was perfect. Kelly was fun to be with and determined to do well.

Hopes for series seven?
After six series, I don't have hopes, I have prayers – and I am far from a religious man! Now, as an old-timer on the show, all I really want is someone who is lovely to be around. We spend so much time in the same space so not to get on is 100 times worse than how well they can cha cha cha, although that does help. Actually, no, I do want someone who can dance too.

What else have you done this year?
I did a travel show called *Intrepid Journey* in New Zealand. I wish it had been cocktails and sandy beaches but it was actually a more hanging-with-the-locals-type travel show, to give you a proper picture. I had a rat run across my face in the middle of the night … Different, very different!

I'm getting married next year and I've had a bit more time to play sports, which I love (surprising, considering I'm not competitive!). Golf, tennis, cricket – you name it, I'm out there.

Voting Explained

Apart from the fantastic dancing, the brilliant costumes and the hilarious antics of John Sergeant, one other event made series six stand out – but for the wrong reasons.

In the semi-finals, an unforeseen result came about when two of the three couples tied, meaning that the third couple, in this case Tom and Camilla, could not avoid the dance-off no matter how many votes they received from the public. Phone voting had to be halted early, with votes either carried over or refunded, while all three couples were put through.

'The BBC did the right thing because they were between a rock and a hard place,' comments head judge Len Goodman. 'If they'd have said you have to go there would have been a furore and the viewers' votes would have been wasted, but they were in trouble because they had to let Tom go through. Of the two evils, they picked the right one.'

In fact, Tom and Camilla were leading the public vote, so it was decided that it was only fair that they should get the chance to compete in the final.

Clearly, something had to be done to prevent this happening again. After several months of looking at various solutions, the BBC identified the problem and came up with the solution. Below is the explanation of the original system, the problem and the modification in the new scoring system.

HOW DID THE ORIGINAL SYSTEM WORK?

Each of the judges awards a mark of between one and ten to each performance so, with four judges, any single dance can therefore earn up to a maximum score of 40.

Once all judges' scores have been awarded, they are converted into points by ranking the couples. For example, where three couples are competing, the couple with the highest score from the judges is awarded three points, the middle couple two points and the couple with the lowest score gets one point.

Once the judges' leader board is finalised, the audience can vote and the couples are ranked according to the actual number of votes received, with the couple receiving the highest number of votes ranked first and the couple with the lowest number of votes ranked last. The ranking is then converted to points so the couple ranked at the top is awarded three points, the couple in the middle two points, and the bottom couple one point.

The judges' points are then added to the audience results to determine the final result. For example, where

three compete, if the couple who are top in the judges' votes are also top in audience votes, their final score would be three plus three, giving them six.

WHY THE PROBLEM OCCURRED

In previous years, when two or more couples tied on the judges' leader boards, they would get an equal amount of points and those below would drop down to the next available points position. For example, with three couples and a tie at the top, as in last year's semi-final, the leading two would receive three points and the bottom couple just one.

Table 1: A previous scenario

Couple	Judges' scores	Judges' points
A	80	3
B	80	3
C	69	1

This meant that, even if the bottom couple received the most public votes, they would only have four points, the same number as the lowest-possible outcome for the other couples, meaning a dance-off was inevitable.

The bottom-placed couple are therefore condemned to the dance-off irrespective of the audience vote – they cannot be saved.

Table 2: The condemned couple

Couple	Judges' scores	Judges' points	Audience votes	Audience points	Grand total	Result
A	80	3	5467	2	5	Saved
B	80	3	4988	1	4	Dance-off
C	69	1	6321	3	4	Dance-off

HOW WILL THIS BE FIXED?

From now on, the couple below two or more tied contestants will receive just one point less than those above them. So, in a three-way battle, where two are tied following the judges' scores, they will both be awarded three points. The remaining couple will now be awarded two points, in contrast to previously, where they would have been awarded one point. This means the gap between the couples has closed so if the audience awards maximum points to the bottom pair, they would be saved from the dance-off, and no couples are safe from the dance-off following the judges' scores, even the couples tied at the top of the leader board.

Table 3: The audience can now save the bottom-placed couple

Couple	Judges' scores	NEW Judges' votes	Audience votes	Audience points	Grand total	Result
A	80	3	5643	2	5	Dance-off
B	80	3	4899	1	4	Dance-off
C	69	2	7564	3	5	Saved*

*Couple C have been saved due to receiving higher audience points than the couple they are tied with overall (couple A).

DOES THIS WORK IF MORE THAN THREE COUPLES ARE COMPETING OR THERE IS MORE THAN ONE TIE?

Yes. With the new system, it doesn't matter how many people are competing or whereabouts in the table they are tied. Table 4 shows the result of a mid-table tie in a six-couple contest. Table 5 then shows the result of a contest where two ties occur.

Table 4: Mid-table tie

Couple	Judges' scores	Old judges' points	NEW judges' points
A	78	6	6
B	76	5	5
C	56	4	4
D	56	4	4
E	34	2	3
F	10	1	2

Table 5: Two sets of couples tied

Couple	Judges' scores	Old Judges' points	NEW judges' points
A	78	6	6
B	78	6	6
C	56	4	5
D	56	4	5
E	34	2	4
F	10	1	3

Even if five couples are tied, and one remains at the bottom, they can still be saved from the dance-off if the public are behind them.

In the next example (Table 6), after the round of judges' scoring, all couples are tied at the top with the exception of one bottom-placed couple. This couple can still be saved from the dance-off by scoring three points or more from the audience.

Table 6: All couples tied except bottom-placed couple

Couple	Judges' scores	Judges' points	Audience points	Grand total	Result
A	78	6	1	7	Dance-off
B	78	6	2	8	Dance-off
C	78	6	4	10	Saved
D	78	6	5	11	Saved
E	78	6	6	12	Saved
F	10	5	3	8*	Saved

*Couple F have been saved due to receiving higher audience points than the couple they are tied with overall (couple B).

What if there is a tie in the grand total at the bottom of the table after the judges' and audience's votes?

In the event that there is no clear result dictating which two couples will go into the dance-off, the couple with the higher audience points will be saved from the dance-off (as shown in Table 7).

Table 7: Audience points take precedence

Couple	Judges' scores	Judges' points	Audience points	Grand total	Result
A	78	6	6	12	Saved
B	78	6	5	11	Saved
C	78	6	4	10	Saved
D	68	4	3	7	Saved
E	70	5	2	7	Dance–off
F	60	3	1	4	Dance-off

DOES THIS MAKE IT EASIER FOR THE WEAKER COUPLES?

Strictly is an entertainment show, and it is now fairer to both the dancers and the audience because the power remains firmly in the hands of the viewer to save or condemn a couple to the dance-off. The revision will only come into effect in the instance of a tie in the judges' marks.

WILL THIS SYSTEM WORK WHEN A GUEST JUDGE JOINS THE PANEL?

Yes, irrespective of how many judges there are, this will not affect the process for how the couples will be ranked following the judges' scores.

You Be the Judge

		Ali & Brian	Lynda & Darren	Joe & Kristina	Natalie & Vincent	Richard & Lilia	Ricky & Erin	Martina & Matthew	Chris & Ola
Show 1	Your Score								
	Judges' Score								
Show 2	Your Score								
	Judges' Score								
Show 3	Your Score								
	Judges' Score								
Show 4	Your Score								
	Judges' Score								
Show 5	Your Score								
	Judges' Score								
Show 6	Your Score								
	Judges' Score								
Show 7	Your Score								
	Judges' Score								
Show 8	Your Score								
	Judges' Score								
Show 9	Your Score								
	Judges' Score								
Show 10	Your Score								
	Judges' Score								
Show 11	Your Score								
	Judges' Score								
Show 12	Your Score								
	Judges' Score								
Show 13	Your Score								
	Judges' Score								
The Final	Your Score								
	Judges' Score								

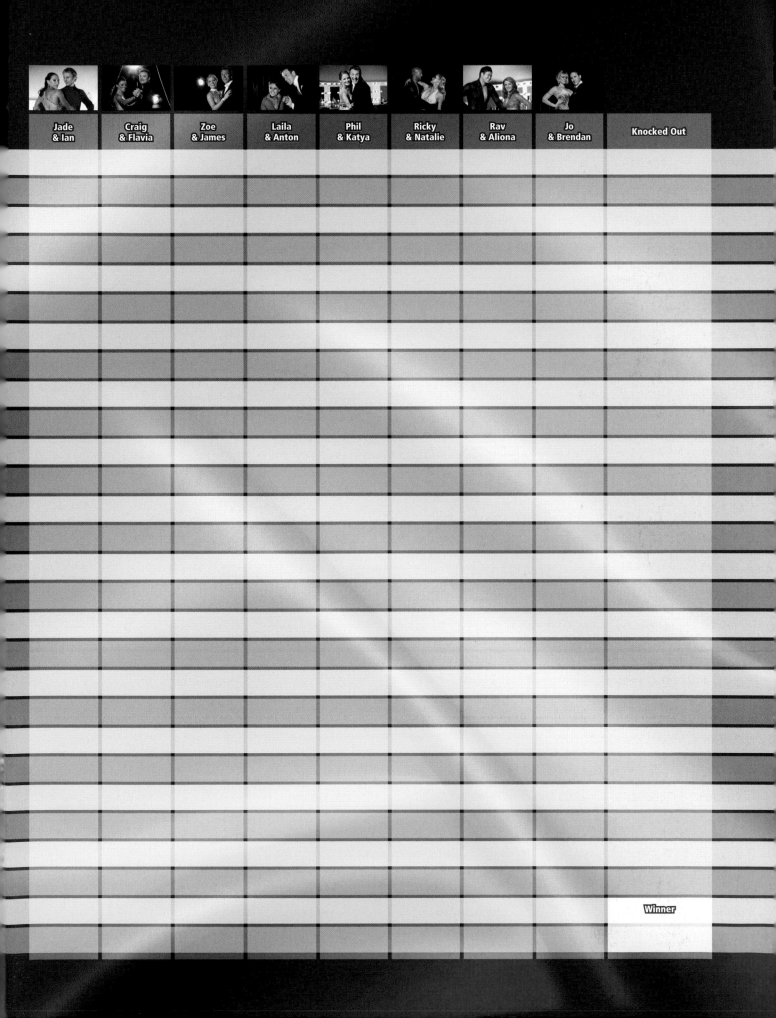

Jade & Ian	Craig & Flavia	Zoe & James	Laila & Anton	Phil & Katya	Ricky & Natalie	Rav & Aliona	Jo & Brendan	Knocked Out
								Winner

Page 10. SCD Expert

1. Darren Bennett 2. Ray Fearon 3. Cape 4. Kenny Logan
5. Nine (Chris Parker, Jill Halfpenny, Patsy Palmer, Louisa
Lytton, Matt Di Angelo, Letitia Dean, Phil Daniels, Gillian
Taylforth and Jessie Wallace) 6. Colin Jackson and Erin
Boag 7. Gabby Logan 8. Jill Halfpenny 9. Series five
10. James Martin 11. Claire King 12. Denise Lewis
13. Nicholas Owen 14. Darren Gough 15. Aled Jones
16. Lesley Garrett 17. Craig Revel Horwood 18. Matt Di
Angelo 19. Lilia Kopylova 20. The cha cha cha 21. A kidney
stone 22. Mark Ramprakash and Karen Hardy 23. John
Sergeant and Gary Rhodes 24. Hanna Karttunen 25. Anton
Du Beke 26. Ian Waite 27. 'Keep dancing!' 28. 40 per cent
29. Brian Fortuna, Hayley Holt and Kristina Rihanoff.
30. 80th

Page 66 Strictly Crossword

Across: 7 Tonioli, 8 Louisa, 10 Mark, 11 Craig, 12 Matt,
13 Len, 16 Sarah, 17 Karen, 18 Ola, 23 John, 24 Roger,
25 Ray, 26 Thorne, 27 Antonia.

Down: 1 Logan, 2 Winkleman, 3 Black, 4 Gough, 5 Jimmy,
6 Karttunen, 9 Ian, 14 Taylforth, 15 Sanderson, 19 Anton,
20 Bruno, 21 Erin, 22 Kylie.

Page 67 Strictly Spot the Difference

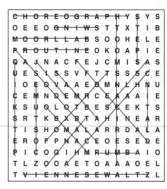

Page 67 Strictly Wordsearch

AMERICAN SMOOTH
BALLROOM
CHA-CHA-CHA
CHOREOGRAPHY
COSTUME
DANCE OFF
FOXTROT
JIVE
LATIN
MAMBO
PASO DOBLE
QUICKSTEP
ROUTINE
RUMBA
SALSA
SAMBA
STEPS
SWING
TANGO
VIENNESE WALTZ

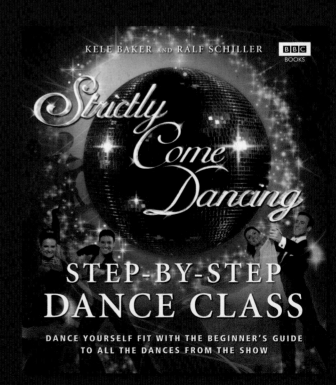